Detecting Deception

Detecting Deception

Tools to Fight Fake News

◆ ◆ ◆

Amanda Sturgill
Elon University

ROWMAN & LITTLEFIELD
Lanham • Boulder • New York • London

Executive Editor: Natalie Mandziuk
Editorial Assistant: Deni Remsberg
Higher Education Channel Manager: Jonathan Raeder

Credits and acknowledgments for material borrowed from other sources, and reproduced with permission, appear on the appropriate pages within the text.

Published by Rowman & Littlefield
An imprint of The Rowman & Littlefield Publishing Group, Inc.
4501 Forbes Boulevard, Suite 200, Lanham, Maryland 20706
www.rowman.com

6 Tinworth Street, London SE11 5AL, United Kingdom

British Library Cataloguing in Publication Information Available

Library of Congress Cataloging-in-Publication Data
Names: Sturgill, Amanda, 1968– author.
Title: Detecting deception : tools to fight fake news / Amanda Sturgill.
Description: Lanham : Rowman & Littlefield, 2020. | Includes bibliographical references and index.
Identifiers: LCCN 2020003474 (print) | LCCN 2020003475 (ebook) | ISBN 9781538141021 (cloth) | ISBN 9781538141038 (paperback) | ISBN 9781538141045 (epub)
Subjects: LCSH: Media literacy. | Fake news.
Classification: LCC P96.M4 S78 2020 (print) | LCC P96.M4 (ebook) | DDC 070.4/3—dc23
LC record available at https://lccn.loc.gov/2020003474
LC ebook record available at https://lccn.loc.gov/2020003475

∞™ The paper used in this publication meets the minimum requirements of American National Standard for Information Sciences—Permanence of Paper for Printed Library Materials, ANSI/NISO Z39.48-1992.

Contents

Preface: Detecting Deception and Why It Matters   vii

Section 1: Distractions and Deceptions   1

1   The Personal Attack: "We Shouldn't Listen to Dummies"   4

2   Poisoning the Well: "Nothing to See Here"   7

3   The Straw Man: "Said No One Ever"   12

4   The Appeal to Hypocrisy: "She Did It First!"   14

5   The Red Herring: "Look! Squirrel!"   17

6   The Black and White: "There Are Only Two Things That Could Happen"   21

7   The Slippery Slope: "And You'll End up Living in a Van by the River"   25

8   The Fallacy of Fallacies: "One Rotten Apple Spoils the Grocery Store"   29

9   The Faulty Analogy: "Comparing Oranges to Falsehoods"   32

10   The Irrelevant Conclusion: "Cool. Don't Care"   35

11   The Hasty Generalization: "I Saw a Thing Once"   38

12   The Division Fallacy: "All the Children Are Above Average"   41

13   The Composition Fallacy: "Great Players Must Make a Great Band"   45

14   Begging the Question: "The Blue Sky Is Blue"   48

15   The Appeal to Purity: "Real Men Don't Eat Haggis"   51

16   Equivocation: "I Mean, I Am Nice"   54

17   The Sunk Cost: "We've Already Invested so Much"   57

Section 2: Unrelated Evidence   61

18   The Appeal to Pity: "If You Really Cared About Me"   63

19   The Appeal to Force: "Agree—or Else"   66

20   The Appeal to Ignorance: "No One Has Proved You Can't"   69

21   The Appeal to Authority: "I'm Not a Doctor But . . ."   72

22   The Appeal to Tradition: "We've Always Done It This Way"   76

23   The Appeal to Popularity: "A Lot of People Agree"   80

24   The Big Lie and Conspiracy Theories: "The Sky Is Green. The Sky Is Green. The Sky Is Green"   83

Section 3: Issues With Numbers and Data   87

25   Ignoring the Base Rate: "100 Percent of People Die"   89

26   The False Cause: "Spider Bites and Spelling Bees"   93

27   The Hidden Variable: "Rabbit Feet and Lucky Rocks"   96

28   Unnecessary Precision: "The Difference That Doesn't Matter"   99

29   Naïve Probability and the Audience It Confuses: "This Slot Machine Is Hot"   102

30   Deception With Charts: "A Picture Is Worth 1,000 Lies"   105

31   Misrepresenting Polls and Surveys: "Four out of Five Dentists Surveyed Agree"   111

Appendix 1: Possible Answers to Section 1 Exercises   117

Appendix 2: Possible Answers to Section 2 Exercises   131

Appendix 3: Possible Answers to Section 3 Exercises   137

References   141

Index   149

Preface

Detecting Deception and Why It Matters

IT'S NOT "FAKE NEWS" to know that journalism is facing a credibility crisis. Journalists talk a lot about checking facts—statistics, history and other little pieces of information that can be true. Failing to report the truth is to risk losing the trust of your audience, to risk discouraging sources from talking to you or to risk getting hauled into court. If you get things wrong a lot, you risk financial ruin. And worst of all, *mistakes in the news business can actually harm real people.*

There's another kind of mistake that we make when we take other people's statements at face value and share them. Whether they accidentally don't make sense or they are intentionally trying to hide a bad idea in worse wording, we need to be careful to not make facts of falsehoods. This book teaches you how to spot problematic reasoning so it can be questioned or corrected. This process is the other half of verification: making sure that statements are logical, reasonable and even possible.

The first principle of the Society of Professional Journalists' code of ethics is to "Seek Truth and Report It." But sometimes it is hard to tell what the truth is. Gatekeepers like journalists had developed methods for fact-checking. Now that anyone can publish in the fast-paced online world, everyone has to check not only facts but also for sense. When a confusing media environment makes it possible for people in the news to say things like, "Truth isn't truth" (Gomez, 2018), it is up to media and audiences alike to detect when the reality presented is misleading or even patently false. Whether you are creating a news package or sharing information on social media, determining what is true before sharing it is an ethical must.

This volume is a practical guide to some of the ways that communicators make facts confusing, ambiguous or just slippery.

Section 1 concerns reasoning issues. From the distraction of a Red Herring to the bad thinking that underlies a Hasty Generalization, intentional or not, reasoning problems make it difficult for the audience to understand the content or the truth.

Section 2 considers ways that communicators mislead their audiences by encouraging them to form opinions for bad reasons. Whether it's because "we've always done things this way" or "everybody thinks so," these arguments encourage emotional decisions instead of rational ones or may even cause the audience to doubt its ability to assess the truth.

Section 3 deals with confusion relating to numbers, which is an area of difficulty for communicators and audiences alike. People's fear of numbers can make them easy to deceive, whether by attributing things to the wrong cause or by creating a chart that hides trends.

Chapters end with opportunities for you to hone your skills at Detecting Deception. You can see real-world examples, find any reasoning problems and try to determine what to do about them. These examples might require verifying the facts or contextualizing the deception for the audience. Suggested answers are found in the appendices at the end of the book.

As you seek truth so you can report it, remember that your job is more than getting the facts straight and the quotes right. It's imperative to find the misleading, distracting and false before publishing or resharing so the audience receives the real news.

SECTION 1

DISTRACTIONS AND DECEPTIONS

◆ ◆ ◆

JOURNALISTS SPEND A LOT OF TIME AND EFFORT on fact-checking and verification and with good reason. It's the bargain that communicators have with their audiences: Audiences give journalists their attention, and journalists provide audiences with the truth. But getting the facts correct is not enough; checking for sense is also important. When a confusing media environment makes it possible for interviewees to say things like, "The president offered alternative facts," it's appropriate to think about *every* possible way that the presented reality might be misleading or patently false.

Sometimes, people deliberately use bad arguments to try to distract from inconvenient facts. What they said may be technically true, but they hope you'll take it the way they presented it. And if you share that misinformation, it is your fault. Consider a company slogan that says a person could save up to 15 percent more than with a competitor. If you repeat that the company saves people 15 percent, that's not what was said. Rather, 15 percent is the maximum, but *up to* 15 includes 1, 15 and all the numbers in between. Because you *could* save, you might not save at all. Candidates, companies and citizens alike will use shady logic and unusual wording in hopes of getting a journalist to repeat or report things that are not true. If journalists get it wrong, they will be called "fake news."

Knowing the ways that people try to be deceptive helps journalists make good choices about what information is worth sharing. It also helps to keep communication focused and based on facts; this knowledge can even help journalists decide against using sources that are trying to control the story. Even better, unraveling deception and providing useful context helps audiences understand the true meaning. Damer (2013, p. 8) suggests that when it comes to sharing someone else's argument, a journalist's job is to capture what the source intends to say. If the source intends to be deceptive, it's better to not share what is said at all. If it must be shared, providing context assists the audience in figuring out the information's value.

This book offers specific examples of how sources can be misleading or unclear. It's not a formal treatment of logic, because, when deciding to use a quote in a story or reshare a story, there is not always time to sketch out a truth table. There are many excellent guides with a more formal approach, but the approach provided here is to develop an awareness of the things sources try so you will know them when you see them. Some general principles come in handy in trying to evaluate the sense of an argument. In general, a good argument will offer at least some evidence to support its conclusion. When people tell you something is true, you should ask yourself three things: What evidence did they offer?

Is that evidence actually related to the point they are claiming? And is that evidence sufficient to prove their point? For example, if I tell you that your neighbor is selling illegal drugs out of her apartment, did I offer evidence? Is the evidence that she has an unusually nice watch? Is it that she has a lot of visitors? Is it that she listens to death metal? Even if all of those are true, do they relate to selling drugs? If they do, is that enough to be proof?

Any argument designed to persuade someone will basically say:

- Because something is true.
- (Add more pieces of evidence, as well.)
- This conclusion is true.

Your job as a journalist is to take these arguments and decide if the evidence is true, if it is related and if it is sufficient to be proof. Remember that an unsupported argument is an opinion, and this needs to be clear to your audience. When people don't have good points to make, they may resort to distraction. They might make fun of others or misrepresent what those others said. It's your job to provide the needed context. For example, one-time presidential adviser Sebastian Gorka told the Conservative Political Action Conference "They want to take away your hamburgers"(Farzan, 2019). Gorka was addressing a dramatic climate change plan called the Green New Deal, and the authors of the article provided context about why the speaker might say that, what the original policy proposal said and even the number of hamburgers Americans eat in a year.

Section 1 considers distraction, using irrelevant information as if it proves a point, making bad assumptions and using misleading language. These issues are sometimes deliberate, but they are *always* deceptive.

1

The Personal Attack

"We Shouldn't Listen to Dummies"

Eloise: We should leave early so we get there in time to get a parking space.

Dwayne: This from the person who is always late to everything. You must be wrong.

DESCRIPTION OF THE ISSUE

In the Personal Attack, you aren't dealing with someone's idea; you are saying it must be wrong because of the person saying it. Even if the person is terrible, that doesn't mean their idea is necessarily bad. Personal Attacks can be against individuals, groups or information sources like publications or websites. Politicians and teenagers alike will use this attack both to avoid considering an idea and to score points against an opponent. That way, not only do they not have to deal with the idea in front of them at the moment, but they also hope the listener will disregard everything from that source into the future. The Latin name for the Personal Attack is *ad hominem*.

EXAMPLE

The accusation of "fake news" is a type of ad hominem attack. An idea that goes back more than 100 years, "the lying press" was a way of discrediting ideas from the news by saying that the media itself was prone to telling lies. Why believe a liar? Author Robert Spicer (2018) writes that the meaning of fake news has evolved recently. Comedians like Jon Stewart, Trevor Noah and Jordan Klepper on Comedy Central often present factual information in a style that imitates cable television's news and commentary shows but is designed to make the viewer laugh as much as to inform them. Media critics called shows like *The Daily Show* and later *Some News* on Cracked.com and *Full Frontal With Samantha Bee* fake news as a way of letting the critics' audiences clearly understand that parody shows shouldn't be expected to adhere to the professional practices and ethical codes found in regular news outlets. With the election in 2016, the meaning of the term began to shift. As Kurtzleben (2017, para 4) noted, the meaning turned to describe news that was simply disagreeable to the person making the statement. Politicians around the world adopted the term. They selectively use "fake news" to suggest that any idea is false because, they claim, the media who report it are inherently untrustworthy. When a news outlet reports things the politician agrees with, those stories aren't called fake. In this way, the politician hopes to become the arbiter of what is credible.

COUNTERING THE PERSONAL ATTACK

Often, a Personal Attack is not worth repeating at all, particularly if sources regularly use dismissive or abusive nicknames for opponents. You should consider carefully whether repeating the statement is likely to confuse the audience. In some cases, repeating a Personal Attack can turn the story away from the issue being considered and into whether the source communicates like a nice or professional person. If the Personal Attack is included as part of a substantive remark, it might be best to paraphrase or excerpt the substantive portion to quote just that, leaving out the attack. For the times when a Personal Attack is relevant, for example if the credibility of the person being attacked is really in question, it's important for you to identify that it is a personal attack along with source's words. You must then supply the context to help your audience to determine how much the person being attacked should be trusted. For example, if an attorney refers to a witness as a liar because the witness was caught lying to police, say that. If the witness would have a unique ability to know something happened, say that too. For example, you might write, "Manning's lawyer said 'Now, ladies and gentlemen of the jury, remember that Mr. Hart here is a known liar.' The lawyer is referring to police charges that Hart lied to officers in the past; however, Hart was the only other person in the store at the time of the robbery."

YOUR TURN

For the following quotations from newsmakers, what is the idea that is being rejected? In what way is the rejection a Personal Attack?

1. US President Barack Obama was working on a deal in which Iran would give up the ability to develop nuclear weapons. In return, the United States and several cooperating European countries would lift sanctions against the country. The deal was quite unpopular in Congress, with all Republicans and some Democrats not supporting it. Talking about the opposition in Congress, Obama said:

    > I've had to make a lot of tough calls as president, but whether or not this deal is good for American security is not one of those calls, it's not even close. Unfortunately, we're living through a time in American politics where every foreign policy decision is viewed through a partisan prism, evaluated by headline-grabbing sound-bites, and so before the ink was even dry on this deal, before Congress even read it, a majority of Republicans declared their virulent opposition. Lobbyists and pundits were suddenly transformed into armchair nuclear scientists. (*Washington Post* Staff, 2019)

    What is Obama saying about his opponents? Is he attacking their ideas or the opponents themselves? If you were writing a story about this speech, how would you contextualize his remarks?

2. In 2004, California Governor Arnold Schwarzenegger was locked in controversial budget negotiations with members of the state's legislature. He was hoping to pressure legislators to come to an agreement using, in part, a humorous gesture. He said:

    > If they don't have the guts to come up here in front of you and say, "I don't want to represent you, I want to represent those special interests, the unions, the trial lawyers . . ." if they don't have the guts, I call them girlie men. (*The Sacramento Bee*, 2008)

    What is Schwarzenegger saying about his opponents? Is he attacking their ideas or the opponents themselves? If you were writing a story about this speech, how would you contextualize his remarks?

2

Poisoning the Well

"Nothing to See Here"

Mr. Lee: Why were you in the restroom so long?

Johan: Well, Lior is going to tell you that I was vaping in there. But he only knows that because he was in there texting the test answers to his friend.

DESCRIPTION OF THE ISSUE

Poisoning the Well is a variant on the Personal Attack, and it happens in advance. The speaker tries to make someone else seem unreliable or irrelevant by sharing something negative about that person before he or she even says anything. You will see this in relation to the media itself when a newsmaker will complain about hypothetical future negative coverage of a decision. In this way, the speaker prejudices the audience toward thinking that media bias is what makes the facts seem negative. This phenomenon can be compelling, so much so that it is taken into consideration in court cases. If a defendant feels that the public information about a crime has been extensive and negative, they may petition the court for a change of venue, which is moving the trial to a location where prospective jurors may not have already made up their minds based on pretrial publicity. Another variation is to present a milder version of negative facts before they come out to get ahead of the story. For example, officials may leak that an employee has been fired for malfeasance. When it comes out that the employee was stealing money, the public will tend to blame the employee and not ask questions about why accounting was not done more carefully.

EXAMPLE

It has been a practice in the US House of Representatives to begin sessions with one-minute speeches. Following a daily prayer and the Pledge of Allegiance, members can ask for unanimous consent to address the body about a topic of the member's choice for a brief period. The Democrats and the Republicans sit on opposite sides of the chamber in the front row, and the two parties alternate the floor for these brief position speeches. As Wolfensberger (2014) describes it,

> Parties like the idea of hitting their C-SPAN audiences early in the day with their catchy messages before eyes glaze over during dense amendment debates.
> I have no problem with the up-front placement of this soapbox derby. Most House members are not in the chamber and pay no attention to it. They are vaguely aware it exists as a kind of partisan purging ritual akin to brushing your teeth. Only in this case it's to prevent the decay of partisan principles. Thus fortified, members can plunge into legislative debates knowing they have at least symbolically warded off Mr. Truth Decay.

This setting of party positions is an example of Poisoning the Well because it creates a partisan lens through which subsequent business can be understood. Here are a couple of examples of one-minute speeches taken from the *Congressional Record* on September 30, 2005, when the House was debating a budget funding resolution to prevent a shutdown.

John Boehner, Republican from Ohio, said:

OBAMACARE NOT READY FOR PRIMETIME

Mr. BOEHNER. Mr. Speaker and my colleagues, as I travel around my district and travel around the country, the American people are worried about their jobs. They are worried about their incomes rising because they are all under pressure. The economy is not growing.

Why isn't it growing?

One of the issues that is standing in the way is ObamaCare—the fact that nobody knows what the rules are. Employers are scared to death to hire new employees and are cutting the hours of many of their current employees.

And for what reason?

This law is not ready for prime time.

The House has done its work. We passed a bill on Saturday night— and sent it to the United States Senate—that would delay ObamaCare for 1 year and would eliminate permanently the medical device tax that is costing us tens of thousands of jobs that are being shipped overseas.

> The Senate decided not to work yesterday. My goodness. If there is such an emergency, where are they?
>
> It's time for the Senate to listen to the American people—just like the House has listened to the American people—and pass a 1-year delay of ObamaCare and a permanent repeal of the medical device tax.

The speeches will be on various issues. Boehner was immediately followed by Jerry McNerney, a Democrat from California.

CLIMATE CHANGE CAUSED BY HUMAN ACTIVITY

Mr. McNERNEY. Mr. Speaker, on Friday, the Intergovernmental Panel on Climate Change published their latest report, confirming that climate change is happening and that it is the result of human activity.

The report was produced by 259 scientists from 39 different countries over the last 6 years, and it is the most comprehensive and authoritative assessment of the Earth's changing climate. The report shows that climate change is real, and it shows the urgency to reduce humankind's CO2 emissions. The scientists now have 95 percent confidence that their findings are correct.

Mr. Speaker, the science is not up for debate. Human-caused climate change is happening. The evidence is overwhelming. Science shows that, if we fail to curb our carbon emissions, we will face catastrophic consequences.

We cannot continue to ignore this overwhelming scientific consensus. Let's work together to reduce our CO_2 emissions and prevent the most severe weather events.

COUNTERING THE POISONING THE WELL

One of the most important ways to counter Poisoning the Well is for a communicator to not be swayed by what is being said. That a person may be biased or untrustworthy may matter, but not in the way Poisoning the Well implies. When speakers try to poison the well, they are hoping that the audience will summarily dismiss the ideas of the person being maligned. Remember that the idea is what is being evaluated. What needs to happen instead is listening to the idea carefully and using extra diligence in seeking confirmation on those same facts. Your job is to understand the ideas and to thoroughly verify those before sharing them. The information that is being used to poison the well may be important to share with the audience, but you must make it easy for the audience to form their own judgment of the information's value. Generally, the attacks should be less prominent than the information shared, and you should make clear how the information was verified, providing that context right in the story.

YOUR TURN

1. In 1960, Senator John Kennedy was running against Richard Nixon, then vice president, for president. Nixon accused Kennedy, who was comparatively younger, of being naïve. At the start of a televised joint broadcast similar to a debate, Kennedy said:

   > Mr. Nixon comes out of the Republican party. He was nominated by it. And it is a fact that through most of these last 25 years the Republican leadership has opposed Federal aid for education, medical care for the aged, development of the Tennessee Valley, development of our natural resources.

   By saying this at the start of the debate, what mindset was Kennedy hoping to evoke about Nixon? If you were a debate moderator, what follow-up questions would you ask of each candidate?

2. Michael Cohen was a longtime personal attorney for Donald Trump before Trump became president. In that role, Cohen was a firsthand witness to many of Trump's financial dealings and was involved in, among other things, arranging a payment of $130,000 to Stormy Daniels, an actress in pornographic films, to secure her silence about a sexual encounter Trump and Daniels had while Trump was married to Melania Trump. The payment happened while Trump was a candidate for president, made to force Daniels to remain silent about the encounter, so her accusation would not hurt Trump at the ballot box. This was illegal under campaign finance laws. Cohen pled guilty and was convicted of a felony for this and other unrelated charges, including lying in a deposition to Congress. After his conviction and prior to his beginning of his sentence, Cohen was called to testify in front of the House Committee on Oversight and Reform. Democrats held the majority in the House and were investigating possible malfeasance on Trump's part and called Cohen because he had in-depth knowledge of the president's actions. Republicans were not interested in investigations that might cause Trump to lose the presidency because a Republican president makes it easier to get laws passed and judges appointed in line with Republican values. All members of the committee were allowed to question Cohen. Prior to Cohen's statements and questioning, the committee chair, Elijah Cummings,

and the ranking Republican, Jim Jordan, were allowed to give opening statements. Jordan began his like this (C-SPAN, 2018):

> Mr. Chairman, here we go. Here we go. Your first big hearing, your first announced witness, Michael Cohen. I want everyone in this room to think about this. The first announced witness for the 116th Congress is a guy who is going to prison in two months for lying to Congress.
>
> Mr. Chairman, your chairmanship will always be identified with this hearing. And we all need to understand what this is. This is the Michael Cohen hearing presented by Lanny Davis. That's right. Lanny Davis choreographed the whole darn thing. The Clintons' best friend, loyalist, operative. Lanny Davis put this all together.

What was Jordan trying to say about Cohen? What evidence did he provide? What context would you want to supply if you repeated Jordan's statements?

3

The Straw Man

"Said No One Ever"

◆ ◆ ◆

Cleveland: I wish it were time for lunch.

Qian: Why do you hate classes so much?

Cleveland: What?!? I'm just hungry.

DESCRIPTION OF THE ISSUE

When someone tries to argue against a position that isn't actually stated, that's setting up a Straw Man. It's a lot easier to knock down a scarecrow than a person just as it's easier to fight an argument when people state their opponents' positions for them. Not only that, the person who sets up the fake argument can look extra brave and virtuous. This is a win-win for the speaker but not for those who have their opposing ideas decided for them. Politicians love doing this because they can set up their policy views to be the most reasonable solution to a problem that they make seem ridiculous. Often, a Straw Man opinion can be attributed to either "many" or "some" people or to a poorly specified group like "liberals" or "conservatives."

EXAMPLE

For example, in 2002, President George W. Bush was working to establish the Department of Homeland Security. It wasn't a smooth process because some members of Congress wanted the employees of the new agency to have the same protections as other civil service employees, and this disagreement slowed the process of approving the new agency. Bush gave a speech in which he said, "the Senate is more interested in special interests in Washington and not interested in the security of the American people," a statement that was met with loud objections from members of the Senate (*New York Times*, 2002). Bush was setting up his own explanation of what the senators believed. It was a Straw Man version of those views: false and easy to attack.

COUNTERING THE STRAW MAN

If someone uses a Straw Man argument, you can try to make this clear by asking the speaker for evidence that the opponent's view is what the speaker claims. In the preceding example, asking the President for specific examples that show the Senate has preferred special interests when it comes to establishing the new department would be a first step. Failing this, it is fair to ask those being misrepresented to review what is being said about them and to give them space in the story to share their opinion. If that is not feasible, you can use your own research and provide that to rebut what is being claimed. For example, if the Senate had done other things in favor of national security such as passing laws or appropriations for other security efforts, those things could be cited.

YOUR TURN

For these quotes from speeches, identify the person whose opinion is being summarized. If you think it is a Straw Man, how would you determine the facts?

1. President Barack Obama, working with a majority-Democratic government, passed the Affordable Care Act. It was the culmination of a hard-fought political battle spanning multiple presidencies and decades. The program was popular with citizens, and eventually about 8 million Americans registered for insurance coverage. "They said no one would sign up," Obama said in a 2014 press conference (Nakamura, 2014).

2. President Bill Clinton was explaining his view that the United States needed to support diplomacy in other countries. He argued that although supporting peacekeeping efforts would take resources from the country, the resulting stability in other countries would pay off in reduced military threat and increased opportunities for trade. "There are people who say, 'Oh, Mr. President, I am for a strong America. I just don't understand why you fool with the U.N. What we need is for America to stand up alone" (Purdum, 1995).

4

The Appeal to Hypocrisy

"She Did It First!"

Charles: You shouldn't take money from your dad's wallet without permission

Charlotte: It's OK. He takes money from my mom.

DESCRIPTION OF THE ISSUE

In the Appeal to Hypocrisy argument, people are saying that what they are doing is acceptable because what someone else is doing is as bad or worse. It is a common tactic in politics, and it often works because the thing the other person is doing is often objectionable. It's also essentially a distraction that is based on faulty reasoning. If you plagiarize on a term paper, but you argue with the teacher that you should not get a zero because everyone else also plagiarized, you are implying that no one should be punished because it's a new norm. The teacher is unlikely to concede, though. Even if you can accuse the teacher herself of cheating, that doesn't mean what you did is acceptable. Even if the teacher loses her job because of the cheating, you should still receive a zero.

You can often spot an Appeal to Hypocrisy argument by the words "what about," a feature so common that "whataboutism" is in the dictionary ("Whataboutism," n.d.), referring to reasoning issues like this. Strictly speaking, whataboutism can be about anyone, whereas an Appeal to Hypocrisy turns the question back to the accuser's own behavior. When presented with an Appeal to Hypocrisy from a newsmaker, it's appropriate to redirect the source in an interview and to disregard it in a speech or document, perhaps making a note to investigate the claim itself as part of a separate story. If a source routinely tries to direct away from the issue at hand by accusing others, avoid live coverage. Quotes can be used in a produced piece in which the reporter can highlight and evaluate the relevant matters. Pointing out an Appeal to Hypocrisy during a live interview and even after the fact can make the journalist seem petty. The Latin name for the appeal to hypocrisy is *tu quoque*.

EXAMPLE

Chappaquiddick is an island in Massachusetts and a political story that has persisted in the American imagination to the point that it was the subject of a 2018 feature film about a 50-year-old mystery. In 1969, US Senator Edward Kennedy was with Mary Jo Kopechne and drove off a bridge to Chappaquiddick Island; the car landed upside down in a pond. Oddly, Kennedy did not report the incident to the police. Questions about what happened and why became a continual source of controversy for the senator, although he remained in the Senate for most of his life. Conspiracy theorists and ordinary citizens alike have found the incident to be a source of questions and suspicion since it happened (Pruitt, 2018).

It's also become synonymous with Appeal to Hypocrisy arguments. Richard Nixon was US president in the 1960s and 1970s, during much of the Vietnam War. He was a controversial president during his time and ultimately resigned under threat of impeachment and removal when media reported that he was directly involved in a break-in at the Watergate office complex. Toward the end of Nixon's presidential career in 1973, Art Buchwald published a humor column in the *Los Angeles Times* titled "Oh Yeah! What About Chappaquiddick" that was a list of 36 comebacks for Nixon supporters to use when people criticized the president (Roy, 2019). Of the 36 suggestions, 5 were to rebut any criticism of Nixon, a Republican, with "What about Chappaquiddick?"—which is an Appeal to Hypocrisy, for sure, as Kennedy was a Democrat.

YOUR TURN

For the following examples, identify which person or group is being accused of what and how they are trying to deflect the focus onto the accuser.

1. When Supreme Court Justice Brett Kavanaugh was in the confirmation process, he was accused of sexually assaulting several women while in high school, most notably Dr. Christine Blasey Ford, a college professor of psychology. The Federal Bureau of Investigation (FBI) conducted an investigation and the Senate Judiciary committee held a hearing, questioning both Blasey Ford and Kavanaugh.

One matter of concern was Kavanaugh's behavior relating to drinking beer, which critics feared might impair his ability to truthfully remember events and provide statements about his high school behavior. Senator Amy Klobuchar questioned Kavanaugh during the hearing, eliciting this Appeal to Hypocrisy response, for which the judge later apologized (MSNBC, 2018).

> KLOBUCHAR: OK. Drinking is one thing, but the concern is about truthfulness, and in your written testimony, you said sometimes you had too many drinks. Was there ever a time when you drank so much that you couldn't remember what happened, or part of what happened the night before?
>
> KAVANAUGH: No, I—no. I remember what happened, and I think you've probably had beers, Senator, and—and so I . . .
>
> KLOBUCHAR: So you're saying there's never been a case where you drank so much that you didn't remember what happened the night before, or part of what happened.
>
> KAVANAUGH: It's—you're asking about, you know, blackout. I don't know. Have you?
>
> KLOBUCHAR: Could you answer the question, Judge? I just—so you—that's not happened. Is that your answer?
>
> KAVANAUGH: Yeah, and I'm curious if you have.
>
> KLOBUCHAR: I have no drinking problem, Judge.
>
> KAVANAUGH: Yeah, nor do I.

Would you report this exchange in a roundup article on the hearing? If so, how would you contextualize it?

2. When actress Roseanne Barr sent a racist tweet about a former Obama administration official, ABC canceled Barr's sitcom, *Roseanne*. That same week, comedian Samantha Bee called President Donald Trump's daughter Ivanka a vulgar name and was reprimanded but not canceled. Ari Fleischer, a former press secretary for George W. Bush, tweeted,

> Compare ABC's reaction to Roseanne Barr's tweet w TBS's non-reaction to Samantha Bee and you'll see a double-standard in action. There's no uprising against Bee. Why? Because she is liberal. Because the MSM protects Obama and his aides, but not Trump. The hypocrisy is sickening. (Yagoda, 2018)

Is Fleischer's tweet newsworthy? If so, how would you report it?

5

The Red Herring

"Look! Squirrel!"

Romeo: You didn't turn in your paper? You're going to fail, and people will think you're a terrible student.

Portia: But I cleaned my apartment!

DESCRIPTION OF THE ISSUE

The Red Herring is when someone tries to distract someone else by throwing out a completely different issue. Usually, but not always, the distracting thing is something that makes the speaker look good. He or she hopes that the listener will follow the bait, and the original issue will be forgotten entirely. Capaldi suggests that if you want to control a conversation, "What you must do is draw attention to a side issue where you feel particularly strong" (Capaldi, 1971, p. 128). When sources use the Red Herring, it can be a clue that they don't feel like they have a defensible position on an issue. It can also be a sign that they haven't really thought through a position yet, so they change the topic to not have to commit. In the face of a Red Herring, it can be difficult to turn the conversation back to the original point. The Latin name for the Red Herring is *ignoratio elenchi*.

EXAMPLE

Red Herrings abound in press releases and statements about bad news. For example, in 2018, United Airlines overbooked a flight scheduled to leave Chicago for Kentucky. Passenger David Dao had already boarded and was seated when he was told he had to give up his seat so a United crew member could get to another flight they were working. When Dao refused to leave, the airline called local police to remove him, and he was dragged, yelling and bleeding, from the plane in an episode that quickly went viral on social media. United CEO Oscar Muñoz addressed the incident for the media by saying "This is an upsetting event to all of us here at United. I apologize for having to re-accommodate these customers" (Levin, 2017). This statement tries to distract from the issue of dragging a passenger by force from a plane by highlighting the other passengers who had their travel disrupted as well—a Red Herring. It was not an effective one, either, because multiple public relations professionals criticized the statement (McGregor, 2017).

COUNTERING THE RED HERRING

In the context of an interview, if someone uses a Red Herring, you can try to redirect them. Acknowledge what they have said ("I hear you saying . . ."), and then add "I'd really like to know your thoughts about . . ." The most aggressive users of the Red Herring will claim that the audience isn't interested in the matter being asked about. For example, if you are interviewing a mayor about police brutality, she may tell you that your listeners don't care about the way arrests work; they care about employment. Even in a live interview, you can neutrally acknowledge that statement as well. "I hear you say citizens don't care about police methods, but still I'd really like to hear your view on it." If someone still fails to answer a question or address an issue, say so in your story or the intro or outro to your package. "The mayor did not answer questions about his management of the personnel budget." It can be valuable to find other ways to learn the person's opinion by asking a spokesperson, conducting a short follow-up interview on just the matter in question or gathering your own background research on the source's previous statements and actions related to an issue, which can be included in the story.

YOUR TURN

1. In 2008, Barack Obama and Hillary Clinton were the final two candidates running in Democratic primaries to be the nominee for President of the United States. In a January debate (CNN, 2008), moderator Wolf Blitzer asked both if they would consider a president/VP ticket with their opponent (either Obama/Clinton or Clinton/Obama). Clinton answered:

This has been an extraordinary campaign, and I think both of us have been overwhelmed by the response that we have engendered, the kind of enthusiasm and intensity that people feel about each of us. And so, clearly, we are both dedicated to doing the best we can to win the nomination, but there is no doubt we will have a unified Democratic Party.

We will go into the November election prepared to win. And—and I want to just add that, you know, on Monday night, I'm going to have a national town hall, an interactive town hall. It will be carried on the Hallmark Channel and on my Web site, HillaryClinton.com, because I know you had tens of thousands of questions. (Transcript of Thursday's . . . , 2008)

Did Clinton answer the question? How would you report her response? No answer? Negative?

2. Mitt Romney became the Republican candidate running against Obama in Obama's first presidential election. In a debate, he was asked about his view on pay equity for women. His response:

Thank you. An important topic, and one which I learned a great deal about, particularly as I was serving as governor of my state, because I had the chance to pull together a cabinet and all the applicants seemed to be men.

And I—and I went to my staff, and I said, "How come all the people for these jobs are—are all men." They said, "Well, these are the people that have the qualifications." And I said, "Well, gosh, can't we—can't we find some—some women that are also qualified?"

And—and so we—we took a concerted effort to go out and find women who had backgrounds that could be qualified to become members of our cabinet.

I went to a number of women's groups and said, "Can you help us find folks," and they brought us whole binders full of women.

I was proud of the fact that after I staffed my Cabinet and my senior staff, that the University of New York in Albany did a survey of all 50 states and concluded that mine had more women in senior leadership positions than any other state in America.

Now one of the reasons I was able to get so many good women to be part of that team was because of our recruiting effort. But number two, because I recognized that if you're going to have women in the workforce that sometimes you need to be more flexible. My chief of staff, for instance, had two kids that were still in school.

She said, I can't be here until 7 or 8 o'clock at night. I need to be able to get home at 5 o'clock so I can be there for making dinner for my kids and being with them when they get home from school. So we said fine. Let's have a flexible schedule so you can have hours that work for you.

We're going to have to have employers in the new economy, in the economy I'm going to bring to play, that are going to be so anxious to get good workers they're going to be anxious to hire women. In the—in the last women have lost 580,000 jobs. That's the net of what's happened in the last four years. We're still down 580,000 jobs. I mentioned 3½ million women, more now in poverty than four years ago.

What we can do to help young women and women of all ages is to have a strong economy, so strong that employers that are looking to find good employees and bringing them into their workforce and adapting to a flexible work schedule that gives women opportunities that they would otherwise not be able to afford.

This is what I have done. It's what I look forward to doing and I know what it takes to make an economy work, and I know what a working economy looks like. And an economy with 7.8 percent unemployment is not a real strong economy. An economy that has 23 million people looking for work is not a strong economy.

An economy with 50 percent of kids graduating from college that can't find a job, or a college level job, that's not what we have to have. (*Politico* Staff, 2012)

Did Romney answer the question? How would you write about his view on pay equity for women?

6

The Black and White

"There Are Only Two Things That Could Happen"

◆ ◆ ◆

Mom: I don't want you on your phone at family dinner.

Inéz: But Mom, I don't want to lose all my friends!

DESCRIPTION OF THE ISSUE

Usually, any one action might have several possible consequences. Black and White thinking falsely assumes that there is only one possible consequence. Sometimes people genuinely lack vision and can only imagine one possibility. In other cases, Black and White statements are a deliberate deception strategy in which speakers want to give an extreme to make what they want seem like the only reasonable course of action. When you encounter Black and White choices, you should wonder if the stated consequence is, in fact, both unique and inevitable. For example, if your professor tells you that you must read the textbook cover to cover or you won't know the material and will fail, it might be good advice. It's not unique advice, though, and failure isn't inevitable. For example, in a journalism class, you might be successful in learning enough rules of AP style by carefully observing examples of style use in the media and following the stylebook on Twitter to pass a course; however, the professor wants you to study the *AP Stylebook* itself and presumes there is no other way you might learn what you need to know.

Black and White fallacies are sometimes used to demand demonstrations of loyalty. Support the principal or you hate your school. Support your senator or you hate the United States. These are relatively easy to identify. It can be trickier to find Black and White fallacies related to particular policies, moral rules or actions.

EXAMPLE

Juvenile curfews are a common place for Black and White thinking. Proponents will frame the curfew as the only alternative to a high crime rate. For example in 2019, Dallas Police Association President Mike Mata addressed a city council committee, "My greatest fear," Mata told the Public Safety and Criminal Justice Committee (Jaramillo, 2019), "is that we allow something like this to expire and we don't reinstate anything else, and we are going to be back here in six months because we are burying dead kids."

The choice he's giving is that either the curfew continues, or the city will have youth who are victims of crime. In truth, there are other alternatives. There are examples in which a curfew is put in place and crime still goes up. In other cases, crime goes down on its own without a curfew. The link between crime and curfews is not inevitable, and this Black and White thinking could keep the city from considering other choices such as jobs programs for teenagers that could also affect the crime rate. In this case, even though the reasoning was flawed, the city council accepted it and reauthorized the curfew.

COUNTERING THE BLACK AND WHITE

All you have to do to refute a Black and White fallacy is to find one additional acceptable alternative outcome that the speaker will agree is possible. Doing this shows that the Black and White choice may not be inevitable. If you hear this kind of reasoning in an interview, you should, at the very least, ask if the source really means there are no other possibilities. In a story itself, often writers can use additional reporting to help make it clear to the audience that there are, in fact, alternatives. If a source says people who don't drink milk hate dairy, a quote with someone who is lactose intolerant can help make the point that there are alternative views and reasons that have nothing to do with hating milk.

YOUR TURN

1. In 2001, the United States suffered a major attack when terrorists flew airplanes into the World Trade Center in New York and the Pentagon in Washington, DC. Immediately afterward, there were statements of shock, support and condolence from many other nations, including the Taliban government of Afghanistan. Later, it become apparent that Osama bin Laden, a Saudi citizen living

in a mountainous region bordering Afghanistan and Pakistan, was behind the attacks. The United States wanted to respond, making it impossible for bin Laden to mount another attack. President George W. Bush was attempting to get other nations to contribute troops to an attack on that region of Afghanistan to deter future attacks. According to CNN, the president said

> Over time it's going to be important for nations to know they will be held accountable for inactivity," he said. "You're either with us or against us in the fight against terror." ("You are either with us . . . ," 2001)

Would you run this quote? How is Bush characterizing other countries? Is this fair? What additional questions might you have for the president to add context to his remarks?

2. In 2015, there was growing global concern about Iran working to enrich uranium and ultimately becoming capable of creating nuclear weapons. The proliferation of nuclear capability has been a concern for many years because the Middle East has historically been politically unstable ("Iran Nuclear Deal . . . ," 2019). Iran was already under economic sanctions from various countries. Along with the United States, several European countries pursued an agreement with Iran's leaders to remove or delay the nuclear threat from Iran. The Iranians agreed to limit their capabilities to develop nuclear technologies and to allow regular outside inspections of their facilities and programs. In return, the outside countries agreed to lift those crippling sanctions. The sanctions had included not having access to foreign markets to sell oil and the return of billions of dollars in Iranian money that had been frozen in overseas bank accounts. In the United States, this move was controversial in an already divided Congress, ("Obama's False Dichotomy . . . ," n.d.) with politicians on both sides of the aisle in disagreement. President Barack Obama gave a policy address in which he said:

> Congressional rejection of this deal leaves any U.S. administration that is absolutely committed to preventing Iran from getting a nuclear weapon with one option, another war in the Middle East. I say this not to be provocative, I am stating a fact. Without this deal, Iran will be in a position, however tough our rhetoric may be, to steadily advance its capabilities. Its breakout time, which is already fairly small, could shrink to near zero.

The choice we face is ultimately between diplomacy or some form of war. Maybe not tomorrow, maybe not three months from now, but soon.

Would you run this quote? What choice is Obama presenting? Is he being fair in his argument? What other questions might you ask and of whom to add context to this statement?

7

The Slippery Slope

"And You'll End up Living in a Van Down by the River"

Raj: I know it's Tuesday night, but let's go catch a movie.

Maria: We can't go out on a Tuesday. If we don't study every night, we'll fail all of our classes. Then we won't be able to get good jobs and we'll end up homeless!

DESCRIPTION OF THE ISSUE

In the Slippery Slope, the argument goes from something real leading to some possible thing, without evidence that the possible thing is certain or even likely. In some cases, Slippery Slope arguments are useful. For example, in legal cases, attorneys and judges will consider the effects of decisions they are making today on future events and actions because they are establishing a legal precedent that can be used to argue future cases. For example, maybe there is a case where the court is trying to decide if the state can specify what types of couples can get married. If it is decided that the state cannot specify, this allows for same-sex marriages, which could be the reason the case was brought in the first place. But if the state doesn't specify, it could also mean adults could marry children, and children could marry each other. Thinking through all of the implications would lead to the conclusion that the law needs to specify something like consenting adult couples. This is a reasonable use of the Slippery Slope.

Some uses of the Slippery Slope are less reasonable. Slippery Slope arguments are often used to persuade based on fear, even when that fear won't happen or is extremely unlikely. For example, an advertisement might use the fear of being friendless. One ad for an air freshener suggested that if the character chose not to purchase it, a smell would move into his or her home, take up residence and get more pungent with time. When neighbors stopped by, they noticed the smell. The implied Slippery Slope is that the neighbors gossiped about it and soon the person who didn't purchase the air freshener wouldn't have any friends. The reverse would be that when someone buys the air freshener, he or she will suddenly become popular—if only it were that easy!

EXAMPLES

Free speech itself has sometimes been the focus of Slippery Slope arguments. A free speech absolutist would say that anyone ought to be able to say anything. It would be up to the audience to weigh the value of what is said and to decide whether to believe it. But even in societies that have free speech as a value, there are usually limits when that speech impedes the rights of others. For example, you might want to freely shout "Gun!" in a crowded stadium whenever you feel like it, even if there was not a gun at all. People could be trampled running away, so this free speech would harm innocent people immediately because there wouldn't be time for the audience to determine that the shout was a lie and not to trust you anymore. Although free speech is a constitutional right, some laws exist that restrict things people can, in fact, say.

A Slippery Slope argument about consequences of speech is sometimes made to limit distasteful speech more than is strictly necessary. For example, Moskowitz (2019) writes about a case in Skokie, Illinois, which in 1978 housed a large population of Holocaust survivors. A Nazi group wanted to have a parade in the town, and the town passed laws including requiring a $350,000 bond for anyone who wanted to march in town and forbade the distribution of materials with swastikas on them. The town's reasoning was that those materials might lead to violence. The American Civil Liberties Union (ACLU) defended the Nazis in court, suggesting the claim that distributing materials with swastikas would lead to violence is a Slippery Slope argument. The *New York Times* agreed ("Nazis, Skokie and the A.C.L.U.," 1978), writing in an editorial that, "the argument that they will provoke violence simply by appearing on the streets of Skokie only emphasizes the obligation of the police to keep the peace—and gives an opportunity for the people of Skokie to demonstrate their respect for the law."

COUNTERING THE SLIPPERY SLOPE

The Slippery Slope is, fundamentally, a chain of cause and effect. The best way to handle it is to unwind the chain, asking about each sequence of cause and effect. In the case of Skokie, where would the violence come from? Would it come from the residents themselves? If so, the *Times*'s argument about showing respect for the law is useful. If outsiders came in and started violent acts, could that be prevented without suppressing speech? What has been tried to accomplish this? These are questions that should be asked for each step as the Slippery Slope is unwound. Is it certain that this will happen? What's your evidence? What might be done to prevent it? What would be reasons this would or would not be done?

YOUR TURN

In the following quotes, what is the first event? What is the final? Is there evidence that the final thing must happen if the first one does?

1. Commentator Sean Hannity responded to a mass shooting in Las Vegas by stating that Democrats and *New York Times*'s columnist Bret Stephens were trying to "undermine the Constitution" by proposing stricter gun restrictions after the event. According to Hannity, Stephens noted that Britain and Australia don't have gun bans but do have gun restrictions. In the column, Hannity said "Good luck to any law-abiding citizen of those countries who wants a gun for protection."

   One of the restrictions proposed in the United States was limiting bump stocks—devices that can modify a gun to shoot more bullets rapidly. Hannity quoted then House minority leader Nancy Pelosi as saying "[Gun rights groups] are going to say, if you give them 'bump stocks' it's going to be a slippery slope." Hannity went on to quote Pelosi as saying "There are many more things members want to do."

   Hannity wrote (2017):

   > They want to ban all guns. They want to disarm millions of law-abiding Americans and prevent them from being able to protect themselves, their children, their wives, their families.

   Was Pelosi right? Is Hannity making a Slippery Slope argument here? To have a news story about this opinion column, what questions might you ask Hannity? What questions might you ask Pelosi?

2. One of the arguments against allowing women to vote in elections was that it would remove a distinctive male contribution to society. Here is a quotation from an anti-suffrage flier ("Anti-Suffrage Flier," n.d.).

Dr. William J. Hickson, head of Chicago's psychopathic laboratory, quoted in From What Will You Be? A Man or a Jelly Bean.

Prohibition is typical of the modern puritan mania. The church movements are also typical. They with prohibition with so called high standard of morality result in a deterioration of masculine physical and mental virility, a falling off of creative ability, of the birth-rate—the latter already noticeable. American pep, which was the result of a masculine-dominated country, will soon be a thing of the past. With the collapse of the male ascendency in this country we can look forward to a nation of degenerates.

What is the first event Hickson notes? What does he say is the final? Is there evidence of a process that will lead to the final thing? How would you contextualize Hickson's comments in a story?

8

The Fallacy of Fallacies

"One Rotten Apple Spoils the Grocery Store"

Jean: All cats are mammals. Fluffy is a mammal. Therefore, Fluffy is a cat.

Claude: Your logic doesn't work here. Therefore, your argument is wrong. Fluffy can't be a cat.

[Fluffy steps out of the litter box, walks over and bites him.]

DESCRIPTION OF THE ISSUE

It's tempting to think that for anything that has parts that are not true, you can then reject the whole thing. When an argument is just erroneous, it would be so convenient to just assume it must be wrong. You can't. At best, a poor argument fails to accomplish its task and persuade. That doesn't mean the premise is wrong, though. It might be right but for a different reason than what is being argued. This is important because one person's bad argument, in some ways, shifts the burden of proof to you because you report the facts. You must then look elsewhere to find evidence for the veracity of the claim.

EXAMPLES

Imagine meeting someone who says they know that Earth is round. You ask them how they know, and they say they saw a globe in a museum, so they knew. However, one could also visit the Museum of the Flat Earth in Newfoundland ("Museum of the Flat Earth," 2018) and see displays of evidence of the Earth being flat. The appeal to authority of the museum is not sufficient evidence. But if you were to say the person's view must be wrong because his or her logic isn't sufficient, and therefore, the Earth must be flat, you'd commit a Fallacy of Fallacies mistake because even though they had a poor argument, the Earth is, in fact, round.

Children learn in grade school that the continents move around on large tectonic plates, but this was not always believed. The notion that there was once a supercontinent, Pangaea, that split into the continents that we know today was boosted through the efforts of a German meteorologist, Alfred Wegener, at the start of the 20th century. Wegener, like early mapmakers, had noticed that the existing continents seemed to fit together like puzzle pieces and proposed a theory of continental drift in which the continents plowed through the crust of ocean basins. Wegener's ideas were rejected by many because although it looked like the continents had moved, he couldn't explain how in a way that could be proven. Geologists at the time, called anti-mobilists, believed that because Wegener's theory couldn't be proven true, it must be false. They rejected Wegener's explanation as wrong and rejected his premise that continents moved—a Fallacy of Fallacy. Their rejection of the method of proof led to an incorrect rejection of the truth ("Historical perspective . . . ," n.d.). Though some "mobilists" persisted, by the 1960s, new types of instrumentation demonstrated that although Wegener's explanation was incorrect, his belief that the continents move was absolutely right.

COUNTERING THE FALLACY OF FALLACIES

When dealing with a speaker who has made a Fallacy of Fallacies mistake, your job is twofold. First, you need to see if they have other evidence for their claim that they are not sharing. They are saying someone or something is wrong because the argument for it is bad. You can even agree that the argument was bad, but then need to ask a question like, "What evidence do you have that the opposite it true?" or "Is there any chance they could be right, but not explaining well?"

Let's say your source is stating that because globes in museums are insufficient proof, the Earth is flat. You could ask, "What evidence do you have that the Earth is flat? Is there any chance that it's round, but they are just not explaining it well?"

Second, you need to do your own investigation to learn the truth of the matter. If you repeat a Fallacy of Fallacies—a claim that a fact is false because there is poor argument for it—your audience needs to know, in the same story, what the truth is and what quality evidence leads to that truth. Any claim will have some evidence supporting it, and some evidence may well be stronger than others. You can acknowledge the problem with the weak evidence and then, restate the strong evidence for the source and ask for commentary on that.

Perhaps you find evidence that the Earth is round, like the fact that ships sailing away from you seem to sink below the horizon and not just get smaller or that the shadow of the moon during an eclipse is a curve. If you find evidence that proves the original bad argument did, in fact, lead to a true conclusion, it's fair to take that evidence back to the same source to ask for commentary.

YOUR TURN

Trying to prove people wrong with a Fallacy of Fallacies argument is a common thing on news site comments and in social-media discussions. Often, a sign of this is when a response is only the Latin name for a fallacy as the comment. Can you find some examples of this poor argument strategy in sites that you read?

9

The Faulty Analogy

"Comparing Oranges to Falsehoods"

Professor: You earned a C+ in this college algebra class.

Stuart: That's not possible. I got As in all of my high school classes, *including* algebra.

DESCRIPTION OF THE ISSUE

It's natural to try to compare things to explain what they are, but when the comparison doesn't match, you may have made a Faulty Analogy. Advertisements are rife with them. For example, babies don't pee blue liquid, nothing you swallow actually coats your stomach and your bathroom cleaner does not, in fact, unleash scrubbing nanobots into your tub (but that might be cool). Two different things won't be exactly the same, of course, but a Faulty Analogy causes issues when the differences are aligned with the substance of the argument. Imagine a nursing student wants to present an argument to his or her professor that an open-book final exam should be given, with the underlying logic being that professionals will, in practice, be able to look up information they don't already know. Even if that is true in some cases, when patients are experiencing severe bleeding, they don't want to wait while their health care professional looks up how to stop it.

EXAMPLE

Government, schools and businesses are organizations. But that doesn't mean that schools should work like businesses or governments. For example, a prime goal in business is to maximize utility—to get the maximum output from the minimum input. You could then generalize and think that massive online courses would be a great model for learning. The professor can put in the effort to develop a course one time and reach thousands of students at once. The analogy doesn't hold up, though. The completion rates for some online courses have been reported anywhere from 3 to 25 percent. It appears that human accountability is an important element for many students. Additionally, a university is not perfectly analogous to a business or to a government—students don't generally elect their bosses or faculty members.

COUNTERING THE FAULTY ANALOGY

When interviewing, asking questions about the parts where the Faulty Analogy doesn't hold up can help. A counter analogy can also be presented to make the point. For example, if a speaker is describing the need for a university to run like a business with the students as the customers, you can ask if employers would appreciate new staff who are ignorant in grammar—a topic students typically dislike and might choose to remove from the curriculum. In a story, it is possible to point out the areas in which the analogy falls short. For example, "Cadwallader suggested that the state university should run like a business, with students as the customer. However, 70 percent of a dollar in educational expenses for a Great U. Student comes from university grants, donors and state support."

YOUR TURN

1. Here is a quote from a CNN story about a presentation that Hillary Clinton made to labor leaders as a candidate in 2007 ("Clinton: 'Rocky and I aren't quitters . . . ,'" 2008).

> Entering to the theme song from the "Rocky" movies, Clinton compared herself to Rocky Balboa, the boxing hero played by Sylvester Stallone, during an address to the AFL-CIO in Philadelphia, Pennsylvania.
>
> "Sen. Obama says he's getting tired of the campaign. His supporters say they want it to end," she said.
>
> "Could you imagine if Rocky Balboa had gotten halfway up those art museum stairs and said, 'Well, I guess that's about far enough'? That's not the way it works," Clinton said, referring to a famous scene in the first "Rocky" movie.
>
> "Let me tell you something. When it comes to finishing the fight, Rocky and I have a lot in common. I never quit," she said.

Clinton may have seen herself as a fighter, but in the movie, Rocky lost that fight. Do you report this quote? In what way?

2. President Lyndon Johnson was having a conversation with the chair of the American Federation of Labor-Congress of Industrialized Organization (AFL-CIO), George Meany (Johnson, 1970, p. 152). Following a discussion about alleviating poverty as a solution for crime, Meany asked if the United States had enough resources to continue to engage with other countries and make progress on domestic issues at home. Johnson answered:

> I am the father of two daughters. When I hear this argument that we can't protect freedom in Europe, in Asia or in our own hemisphere and still meet our domestic problems, I think it is a phony argument. It is like saying I can't take care of Luci because I have Lynda Bird. We have to take care of both of them and we have to meet them head on.

Did Johnson address Meany's concern? What follow-up questions might you ask to determine the answer?

10

The Irrelevant Conclusion

"Cool. Don't Care"

◆ ◆ ◆

Sheila: Don't eat that berry; it's poisonous.

Guy: Nah, it can't be. See how appetizing it looks?

DESCRIPTION OF THE ISSUE

Sometimes a conclusion is true but not important. The speaker hopes that the evidence he or she presents relates to the matter at hand, but it does not, and this can be hard to catch in conversation. It is a common tactic in politics and for lawyers in court. In politics, when a candidate is asked about qualifications in one area, he or she may answer with qualifications in another area, hoping that the listener will think being qualified in one area implies qualification in others. But just because someone is good at algebra does not mean he or she is also a good speller. In legal settings, attorneys may try to sway a jury by describing the nature of the crime. That being beaten is brutal and greatly affects a victim may be true but it isn't relevant to whether a defendant was the perpetrator. A building may be poorly maintained, but that doesn't necessarily mean that the management is responsible for a faulty space heater in the lobby that caused a fire. This will sometimes also be known as *ignoratio elenchi*.

EXAMPLE

As a response to several controversial police killings of unarmed minorities, a movement called Black Lives Matter advocated for dialogue and action toward what members felt was more equitable treatment under the law. In the face of this, some groups who thought the movement was badly conceived starting using slogans like Blue Lives Matter in support of police and All Lives Matter to suggest it is inappropriate to single black citizens out. This is an example of an Irrelevant Conclusion. It is true that police lives matter and that all lives do. However, in the face of the high-profile deaths of black citizens, the statements are beside the point that the deaths of black citizens at the hands of law enforcement are worth investigating.

COUNTERING THE IRRELEVANT CONCLUSION

When faced with an Irrelevant Conclusion, it is beneficial to clarify with sources whether the first thing implied is actually evidence for the second. If a spokesperson says you should vote for his or her candidate for state representative because they were a strong military leader, don't just take that for granted. You need to ask for specifics about military leadership in general and about the candidate's record as a military leader. You also need to investigate the qualifications of a good representative. Are the leadership skills the same? It is helpful to get some of these assessments from neutral third parties. If the qualifications are not the same, ask the spokesperson to clarify why he or she thinks that the candidate is qualified, because the military leadership may be interesting but unrelated to the job being sought.

YOUR TURN

1. Some people frame changes of positions as a bad quality in an elected official because some voters expect a candidate to make decisions in office that are in line with what the candidate did in the past. When Mitt Romney was running for president, debate moderator John Harwood asked him about changing his opinion on matters.

> Your opponents have said you switched positions on many issues. It is an issue of character, not personal, but political.

Romney's reply began:

> I think people understand that I'm a man of steadiness and constancy. . . . I have been married to the same woman for 25—excuse me, I will get in trouble, for 42 years. (CNBC, 2011)

> Did Romney address the concern or did he present an Irrelevant Conclusion? Would you report this quote as an answer to the question?

2. In 2019, the board of trustees of the University of South Carolina was hiring a new president. After they did not agree on a candidate in the spring, the board came together in a surprise move the following summer to vote on former West Point superintendent Robert Caslen. The move raised questions from faculty and alumni, and in the face of some resistance, an anonymous Twitter account began sharing information in favor of Caslen, including the following:

> @Caslen4President
> Those against Caslen for President of USC are focused on him not having a Ph.D. They fail to mention he has two masters degrees, is one of only 23 generals of his rank and was one of the most successful superintendents at West Point in history. #Choosecaslen #usc #obviouschoice

Does this tweet represent a relevant conclusion? If you were using the tweet as a story about Caslen's controversial hiring, what context would you provide?

11

The Hasty Generalization

"I Saw a Thing Once"

Shannon: French people are so intolerant of tourists who don't speak the language!

Kerry: How do you know?

Shannon: I had this waiter in Paris who was so rude when I couldn't figure out the menu.

DESCRIPTION OF THE ISSUE

The Hasty Generalization is drawing a conclusion without having enough evidence to draw that conclusion; a few cases are mistaken for a bigger trend. You can see this several ways. Sometimes, the speaker doesn't have much data at all. If I go to a new city and try to catch a bus and that bus is late, it would be a Hasty Generalization to assume that all buses in the city run behind. Sometimes, the speaker has chosen a few events, but the events they have chosen are exceptional. You'll see this in bad assessments of dramatic things happening. If a person is attacked on the Appalachian Trail, it can seem like the trail is a dangerous place and should be avoided. When you consider how many people hike on the trail each year (estimated at more than 2 million by the Appalachian Trail Conservancy), it doesn't seem that dangerous anymore. Notice that the media itself can contribute to these kinds of Hasty Generalizations about risk as they choose to highlight attacks when they happen. Hasty Generalizations are not always innocent. Sometimes sources will deliberately choose to draw conclusions from a biased set of data to create a situation that seems to be based on facts, but is in fact favorable to them. Essentially, they are intentionally misusing the data to be deceptive. In Latin, this is known as *dicto simpliciter.*

EXAMPLE

Although the great majority of scientists agree that global warming is a real phenomenon, some sources forget this in the winter when there is a cold snap where they are. On February 26, 2015, Senator James Inhofe from Oklahoma made this point with a prop on the Senate floor. "In case we have forgotten, because we keep hearing that 2014 has been the warmest year on record," he began, "I asked the chair, 'Do you know what this is?' It's a snowball from just from outside here. So it's very, very cold out. Very unseasonable." Behind him stood a large photograph of people standing next to an igloo they had built, and he gave other examples like seeing photos of rapid ice buildup on the Great Lakes. He went on to give a policy speech about the "hysteria" about global warming detracting from interest in global terrorism as a threat. The snowball and photo were used as data to begin an argument that global warming is not a serious problem (Bump, 2019).

Climate change is a much more complicated issue than local weather, and reporting needs to make this clear. The bizarreness of the snowball gag does have some news value and seemed to work, as it was included in a story about the debate. However, it should not be a central point but could be added as context. For example,

> Senator James Inhofe of Oklahoma argued that climate change was being given too much focus in public policy making. He illustrated that with a snowball in a plastic bag that he brought to the chamber floor, noting that its existence illustrated the fact that it was "very, very cold" outside the building. This cold, he implied, demonstrated that concerns about climate change were "hysteria." Scientists agree that climate change does not mean that all places will uniformly be warmer. The fact that it was cold in D.C. yesterday doesn't have any bearing on whether climate change exists.

COUNTERING THE HASTY GENERALIZATION

It's vital to not accept information or data at face value. If sources do not indicate how they got the facts for a given conclusion, it's appropriate to follow up on your own with the source, the original source of the data, or with both. If a source is adamant about a pattern existing that is not supported by the examples provided, you should not simply quote them but, rather, provide context for the reader in the same piece. If someone gets up at a city council meeting and says, "You need to do something about the growing crime in our city. Just this year, five of my neighbors have had break-ins," you need to provide context for the reader. Ask the speaker what is meant by this year, since it could be January or the previous 12 months, and then find out and include statistics over time for that neighborhood and for the entire city. If someone tells the school board that crowded schools are causing discipline problems, you need to get data on the changing populations at those schools and on the rate of discipline incidents. Whenever you are drawing conclusions from experience, context matters.

YOUR TURN

1. In a 2000 presidential debate ("October 11, 2000 Debate Transcript," 2000), candidates George W. Bush and Al Gore were asked for their views on gun control. Gore said all states should license handguns because "too many criminals are getting guns. There was a recent investigation of the number in Texas who got—who were given concealed weapons permits in spite of the fact that they had records," citing a *Los Angeles Times* article. Could you use Gore's quotation as a part of a story about criminal access to guns? What are his assumptions about gun permits given to criminals based on? What additional reporting would you need to do before writing a story based on his claim?

2. When Ronald Reagan was running for president in 1976, a fixture of his campaign speeches was welfare reform. In particular, he repeatedly mentioned a Chicago woman who exemplified people getting rich off public benefits. At a campaign rally in Guilford, New Hampshire, he said ("Welfare queen becomes issue . . . ," 1976)

> There's a woman in Chicago. She has 80 names, 30 addresses, 12 Social Security cards and is collecting veterans' benefits on four nonexisting deceased husbands. And she's collecting Social Security on her cards. She's got Medicaid, getting food stamps and she is collecting welfare under each of her names. Her tax-free cash income alone is over $150,000.

What is the point Reagan is trying to get the audience to believe? Does he provide sufficient evidence of a welfare abuse problem? Before printing Reagan's remarks, what questions might you want to ask him? What kinds of background research could you do to add context to these remarks if you decide to share a post or include them in a story?

12

The Division Fallacy

"All the Children Are Above Average"

◆ ◆ ◆

Pramila: *Saturday Night Live* is the best show on TV. But I don't understand why this week's opening sketch wasn't funny.

Diego: You can't win them all.

DESCRIPTION OF THE ISSUE

In the Division Fallacy, an attribute of a group is assumed to be true of everyone or everything in it. If a basketball team does well, most people figure all of the players are great shooters because people assume that anything great must have equally great parts. For example, imagine that at the end of a group project, the group gives an amazing presentation. A classmate says if your team creates a fantastic presentation, every person on your team must also be capable of giving a great presentation on his or her own. If you've ever worked on a group project, you know this is seldom the case—that's a reason people do things in teams. You expect that some group members will bring different strengths, and their uniqueness makes for a better overall project. You can also see it in things people say about opinions. A speaker might say all Americans, Muslims, veterans or another group share a common belief. It is not just an issue with people. It can apply to things as well. For example, you might think that all of the ingredients in a tasty dish would be, themselves, delicious. Until you try to eat the salt. This logic problem is easy to create, but it's also relatively easy to counter.

EXAMPLE

The *Today Show* ran an article on celebrity siblings (Hines, 2008), featuring unknown actors like Daniel Baldwin and Ali Lohan, who were from the same family as more prominent siblings Alec and Lindsay. Hines writes:

> No other celebrity family encompasses the there-to-nowhere scope of fame quite like the Baldwins. A-list brother Alec leads the pack, B-list Billy comes in a distant second, and somewhere between reality TV fixture Stephen and complete obscurity lies Daniel.

This quote and other writing in the article is assuming that because the family is notable in acting, all the parts—in this case each of the brothers—should be notable actors as well. This is a Division Fallacy. Just because a choir sounds good doesn't necessarily mean that each singer is equally skilled as a soloist.

COUNTERING THE DIVISION FALLACY

The Division Fallacy is best countered by asking for supporting evidence. Just because many presidents have had an Ivy League legal education doesn't mean they are skilled attorneys. If someone claims this, ask for evidence specific to the question like important legal victories. It may help to give a blatantly ridiculous example of this fallacy. For example, New York is a financial capital of the United States. Therefore, everyone who lives in New York must be rich. If evidence is not provided, state that in your story. "Sanchez said Professor Smith is qualified because the university has excellent rankings; therefore, each of the teachers is excellent. She did not provide evidence for Smith's teaching record."

YOUR TURN

1. In 2018, the US government was dealing with some large groups of migrants arriving at the southern border and asking for asylum because, the migrants said, conditions in their home countries meant they could no longer live there safely. Developing a plan to deal with a large number of migrants and sorting out who had legal claims to asylum overwhelmed existing border patrol programs. This became one of the most controversial sets of policy decision and action surrounding the Donald Trump administration at the time. Things came to a head in the fall with nationwide protests over policies

like separating children from the family members with which they crossed the border and holding them in separate detention facilities. In November of that year, Trump gave a national address seeking to justify actions on the border. Trump said (Trump, 2018),

> I don't want them in our country. And women don't want them in our country. Women want security. Men don't want them in our country. But the women do not want them. Women want security. You look at what the women are looking for. They want to have security. They don't want to have these people in our country.

What are the assumptions that Trump was making in that statement? Which one may be subject to the Division Fallacy? Is there another fallacy at play here as well? What kind of evidence would you ask for in support of this statement?

2. The 21st century saw a return of some childhood diseases like measles and mumps in the United States and abroad. Although vaccines do exist for the diseases, growing numbers of parents are refusing the vaccines for their children. Researchers who have studied vaccine hesitancy have uncovered a variety of reasons for rejecting the shots, including religious belief, worry that the shots cause damage and a concern that mandated vaccines represent the government overreaching into control of what people choose to do with their bodies. It's been a frustrating problem for government because fewer vaccinated people means more people get disease. There is a small number of people for whom vaccines are actually medically dangerous. If more people who can get shots refuse them, resulting in more disease, those who are medically fragile are at greater risk of getting and dying from preventable causes. A few states that had larger outbreaks sought to increase the pressure on parents to vaccinate their children by doing things like excluding unvaccinated children from public schools. Some states considered state review boards to evaluate physician claims that their patients' health precluded vaccination.

California was one such state. As the California state legislature debated requiring oversight of exemption claims, one state senator, a Sacramento pediatrician named Richard Pan, chair of the Senate health committee, said:

> Clearly we're going to have to contend with the large number of people who, unfortunately . . . are misinformed about vaccines.

And that's in the backdrop of all the measles outbreaks that are happening all around the U.S.

Some patients are misinformed about vaccines when it comes to dangers like getting some diseases from their vaccines. Does belonging to the group of parents who are against vaccinating their children mean that they are misinformed? Is this an example of the Division Fallacy?

13

The Composition Fallacy

"Great Players Must Make a Great Band"

Rob: What flavor of ice cream did you make?

Xu: I put in all my favorite flavors: Coffee, raisin, peach, mint, orange, chocolate. It should taste great!

DESCRIPTION OF THE ISSUE

The Composition Fallacy assumes that because component parts are good, the whole must also be good. If you are taking a course in great works in literature, each is considered to be notable, so you might assume that the course would therefore be great. This is not necessarily true because the professor, the structure of the course or the other students might affect the final course. When people make this fallacy, they are ignoring the way that the parts might affect one another that changes the character of the whole. Even when citizens elect qualified representatives to legislative bodies, those bodies do not always work together effectively. The reverse issue can be true as well; sometimes groups with bad members still do good things. Just because prisoners pick up trash on the side of the road doesn't mean the roadside isn't cleaner when they are done.

EXAMPLE

It is tempting to make a Composition Fallacy when talking or writing about sports. Consider Olympic teams where competitors are highly accomplished individually in the sport. For example, the Bleacher

Report website (Knox, 2012) wrote about the US Olympic basketball team, saying:

> The 2012 Olympics are right around the corner and Team U.S.A. should be ready to take on the best that the basketball world seemingly has to offer.

The team featured NBA standouts like LeBron James, Kobe Bryant and Kevin Durant, who were all well-known and decorated players at the time. But basketball is a team sport, and composing a team can be a different matter. The 2012 team did take the gold medal, but that can't be assumed. The 2004 team featured two members who had earned NBA's most valuable player and still came in third. The same can be true in arts, where several excellent solo voices can make a poor choir.

COUNTERING THE COMPOSITION FALLACY

In an interview, you can point out an obvious case where the parts don't add up to a great whole. You might have a great swimsuit top, elegant tuxedo pants, a sturdy pair of work boots and a gorgeous diamond tiara, but when you put them together, it's a pretty strange outfit. You can then ask the speaker for evidence that the parts described will all interact well. If you don't have the opportunity to do interviews, note in the article that the speaker is assuming that the good or bad parts make a good or bad whole, but that there isn't proof that is true.

YOUR TURN

1. In 2008, Olga Franco, an undocumented immigrant, killed four children in a traffic incident that led to her conviction for vehicular homicide. Michelle Bachmann, a candidate running for re-election to the House of Representatives, used the tragedy as an example in favor of curbing immigration by suggesting Franco was an example of the problems with illegal immigrants. On *The O'Reilly Factor*, a Fox News TV show, she was talking with host Bill O'Reilly about the incident and said:

   > This is a crime problem. This is an issue of anarchy versus the rule of law, and the question is when are we going to get serious about this and stop tinkering around the edges. If we can't get serious and outraged about four innocent kids, one of which will be buried tomorrow, I don't know what it's going to take.

Bachmann used the accident in other campaign events to highlight what a Minnesota Public Radio reporter described as "the problem with illegal immigrants" (Pugmire, 2008).

Are the actions of one immigrant enough to determine the reputation of all or to make policy? Can you find evidence of the crime rate for undocumented persons to compare with that of citizens in the United States? How would you handle this in a story?

2. In a column about police brutality, columnist Rashad Robinson (2019) wrote,

> One idea we must reject is the idea of trusting law enforcement to protect us from white nationalist violence, given how much they contribute to it. If people in law enforcement want to be seen as experts on defeating white nationalism, shouldn't they have to get rid of all the white nationalists in their own ranks first?

Is it reasonable to say this? Does the presence of white supremacist members of police forces mean that police as a whole cannot be trusted? If someone made this claim in an interview, what follow-up questions would you ask them?

14

Begging the Question

"The Blue Sky Is Blue"

◆ ◆ ◆

Sophia: The dance was really fun.

Brandon: Why do you say that?

Sophia: I had a good time.

DESCRIPTION OF THE ISSUE

Begging the Question means assuming the thing you are trying to prove is already true. When that is done, there isn't a question. If I say something like, "We know the sky is blue because it is blue," this is obviously ridiculous. When speakers beg the question, it can be difficult to detect because sometimes the wording around the question or the conclusion is changed. Consider, "This college has harsh punishments for student drinking. Students who get caught can get suspended." That is a possible punishment, but that, in itself doesn't prove it is harsh. A special thing to watch for is the leading question, where the way the question is asked implies the correct answer. "You wouldn't want an exam the Monday after Spring Break, would you?"

EXAMPLES

Pessin and Engel (2015, p. 114) report a classic example of Begging the Question in which Calvin Coolidge, who was seeking office, reportedly said, "When large numbers of people are out of work, unemployment results." In that unemployment is the same thing as being out of work, this is obvious and meaningless. Coolidge's writings and speeches make it apparent that he was a strong advocate for personal responsibility as a way of avoiding excessive government. It's possible what he meant is that when people choose not to work, society must deal with the consequences of unemployment, but that's not what he said. This has persisted as an amusing example for nearly 100 years. Listeners and reporters at the time would have done well to ask for a follow-up to explain the context.

In 2004, President George W. Bush was speaking at a journalism convention ("George W. Bush on the tribal sovereignty," 2004), and said, "Tribal sovereignty means just that; it's sovereign. You're a—you've been given sovereignty, and you're viewed as a sovereign entity." These are silly examples but also show that sometimes even people in high positions speak in this way.

COUNTERING THE BEGGING THE QUESTION

When people beg the question, it's possible that they are trying to be deceptive, but it's also possible that they are being careless with their expression but have another intended meaning. You should make an honest effort to determine which is meant and include that context when it is shared or published. If a follow-up question is possible, pointing out the meaninglessness of what was said can be helpful in giving the person a chance to restate it in better language. If follow-up questions aren't possible, you can point out the meaninglessness of the statement. If it seems like the speaker didn't mean it the way it came out, you can suggest that. When you share that person's other statements, say that they might have meant something else, but you could not confirm it. It's important to make things clear for the audience, and it is ethically questionable to repeat unfortunate wording for humor.

There are also examples of name-calling that essentially beg the question. For example, during the 2016 campaign, candidate Donald Trump called his opponent, Hillary Clinton, "Crooked Hillary." Similarly, columnist Molly Ivins called Rick Perry, a governor of Texas who later went on to be Secretary of Energy, "Governor Goodhair," as a way of suggesting that Perry had the look of a politician but lacked the brains (Suebsaeng, 2017). Both of these kinds of statements are using the person's description as a statement about the person's characteristics. However, there is no evidence for corruption on the part of Clinton or for poor thinking on the part of Perry that could be proven simply by name-calling. It is best to avoid repeating or quoting these kinds of statements entirely.

YOUR TURN

1. Florida Senator Marco Rubio ran for the Republican nomination for President of the United States against a large field of 17 candidates who participated in at least one debate. In February, in the middle of the primaries, he was giving a campaign speech and said the following ("Rubio bashes Trump," 2016):

> When you make me president, when you make me president, we are going to have a president that embraces a free economy. Free enterprise works, I know it, because my parents, we're not rich people. My father was a bartender and my mother was a maid. And the reason why they had a job is because free enterprise works. Because someone who had access to money risked that money to open up a hotel and hire them.
>
> Free enterprise works because it is the only economic model in the world where you can make poor people richer, and you don't have to make rich people poorer. We are going to save free enterprise.

Is Rubio Begging the Question? If so, what is he assuming is true without providing evidence? Would you directly quote this segment of his speech? Why?

2. Many presidents will address the fact that elections are never unanimous by trying to point out that the nation now needs to come together around values everyone can agree on. When John F. Kennedy was inaugurated (Kennedy, 1961), in his inaugural address, he said: "United, there is little we cannot do in a host of cooperative ventures." Is Kennedy making a profound statement, or is he Begging the Question? What is his evidence for the might of unity? How would you contextualize this statement?

15

The Appeal to Purity

"Real Men Don't Eat Haggis"

Shaun: I don't have a flag for Flag Day.

Jon: A true American would have remembered to buy one in advance.

DESCRIPTION OF THE ISSUE

Maybe real men *would* eat oats stuffed in a sheep's stomach, but no person from Scotland would put sugar on their oatmeal or lemon in their tea. In an Appeal to Purity, the speaker argues that someone is out of the relevant group because he or she believes something or does something that the *true* (e.g., citizen, patriot, Christian, Jew, Muslim, East High School Wildcat, etc.) would do. Real feminists are vegan because eating milk is abusive to female animals. Real Christians reject evolution. Real Wildcat fans don't leave at halftime. The purpose of an Appeal to Purity is to create in-groups and out-groups. The listener believes people are in the in-group because of a belief or behavior or that people's ideas should be rejected because they don't hold the belief of in-group. An Appeal to Purity is sometimes called the "No True Scotsman" fallacy.

EXAMPLE

As the US political landscape has gotten more contentious, we've seen the rise of Republicans in name only (RINO) and Democrats in name only (DINO); they are names that more extreme members of a political party will call more moderate members. Commentator Ken Braun published a column (2013) in which he states that the Tea Party, a conservative political group, was calling New Jersey Governor Chris Christie a RINO. Christie got the moniker for doing things like expressing appreciation to a Democratic president who visited to assess hurricane disaster relief and for not being sufficiently hostile to gay marriage and gun control. Braun also mentions Joe Lieberman, who, as a Democratic vice-presidential candidate, was criticized for supporting a Republican president on national security issues. The -INO affiliation is intended to show a failure of a doctrinal purity test in which there is no room for compromise or consideration of opposing views. It's an Appeal to Purity.

COUNTERING THE APPEAL TO PURITY

In an interview context, it may be possible to encourage the speaker to focus on issues by asking for commentary on the issue in particular. In text, if the speaker doesn't address issues, it's useful for the reader for you to do that. Although Appeals to Purity often sound like powerful quotes to include in your piece, select quotes with a focus on the issue being discussed. In the -INO example, you can talk about how people who use that name tend to come from more extreme wings of their respective parties. You can then explain about the differences in beliefs that are found within the Democratic or the Republican parties. In this way, readers understand the issues and aren't distracted by an unsupported attack.

YOUR TURN

1. Controversies over the need to verbally support the US government didn't start with burning the flag during the Vietnam War or, more recently, with kneeling during the National Anthem. The *Congressional Record* for 1936 includes a speech entered by Mississippi representative Aubert Dunn, ("Proceedings of the 18th National Convention of the American Legion . . . ," 1936) who argues:

> I think no true American, however warped his mind may be as concerns party faith and principles, will deny that the first duty we owe our government is that of moral support. That we should defend it against those that wrongfully assail it with words.

> He goes on in the speech, which he had given to the District of Columbia Democratic Club on George Washington's Birthday, to argue that criticizing the government is harmful because it causes people to doubt the government, which then makes the government less effective.

2. In the early 1990s, large numbers of political asylum seekers from Haiti began arriving in the United States in boats, fleeing what they said was political persecution. Repatriation, which is sending people back home, had been the national policy for many years but moved slowly because the situation in home countries was not improving. The large number of impoverished people arriving was stretching resources in some cities and states; thus, the government began housing migrants in secured camps near Guantanamo Bay in Cuba, with numbers growing to more than 10,000. As the administration began considering mass repatriations, there were congressional hearings to discuss "The Haitian Refugee Crisis." In those hearings, California Representative Vic Fazio argued in favor of US support for Haitians (Fazio, 2019), saying:

> I agree that we cannot afford to open our doors to all the poor people of every nation who want to enter the United States to better their lives. But Haitians do not want this. They want to be able to live in their own country, in a democracy, where their basic human and civil rights are respected. When this was the case, Haitians were not setting sail for the United States.
>
> But we all know that this is not the current situation. When last September's coup shook the island of Haiti, its democratically elected Government was overthrown, its President was forced into exile, and the military took over. Over 1,500 Haitians were killed, and thousands more began to flee their country, fearing for their lives.
>
> The Haitian people have two very limited options. They can remain in Haiti, where the military now rules with an iron hand and where supporters of democracy face torture, and even death. Or they can risk death on the high seas, as they attempt to seek refuge here in the United States.
>
> We cannot continue to turn our backs on these people. It is cruel. It is inhumane. It is heartless. It is wrong. Madam Speaker, I commend my colleague from Michigan, Mr. Conyers, for calling this special order and for not allowing us to forget the plight for our Haitian neighbors. I urge my colleagues on both sides of the aisle to revisit this issue so that we, as true Americans, can demonstrate our commitment to fairness, justice, and basic human rights.

What is Fazio saying about Americans? What could be other views that Americans would have on migrants? If you were writing a story about this, who else would you interview for a holistic view?

16

Equivocation

"I Mean, I Am Nice"

◆ ◆ ◆

Helena: Why wasn't my song on your playlist?

Hector: What are you complaining about? You told me to drop it at my next DJ job.

DESCRIPTION OF THE ISSUE

One technique people will use when the are being deceptive is Equivocation, which is using a word with multiple meanings, hoping that listeners will believe one definition is meant, while speakers can claim they meant another definition.

A car salesman did this once. He told the customer he was lucky he came in that day because they were having a public sale. This was great news because sale means a discount, right? Well after the test driving and the "talking to the manager" and all that, the customer expected to pay less than the sticker price. So, um, what about the sale? "Oh, that just means we're selling them to the public." The salesman was equivocating because sale also just means taking money in return for a good. The customer was irritated because he had spent all day expecting that he'd get a discount price on the car.

A humorous example of this was a campaign in 2019 in South Dakota that hinged on Equivocation to get its point across (Kesslen, 2019). Methamphetamine addiction was a serious problem in the state and the campaign wanted to get across the idea that fighting meth was everyone's problem. A series of public service announcements (PSAs) and billboards showed individuals and groups of people with the words, "Meth: We're On It." This was highly memorable because of Equivocation. "On it" could mean currently under the influence of a drug, or it could mean on top of the matter. The agency that created campaign said the Equivocation was deliberate.

EXAMPLE

President Bill Clinton was impeached in 1998 for lying under oath and obstructing justice in a highly watched case related to his conduct in a sexual harassment lawsuit. Paula Jones's attorneys wanted to prove that the president had had a pattern of harassing behavior toward women, and they found information about a sexual relationship Clinton had with a White House intern. Clinton gave a sworn deposition to the court denying he had the relationship or even knew the woman. According to an independent counsel report, Clinton asked his secretary to help cover for him, constituting obstruction of justice, which is a serious crime.

In the process, when Clinton testified in front of a grand jury, he was asked why he gave a false statement in the deposition, and Clinton replied "It depends on what the meaning of the word 'is' is. If the . . . 'is' means is and never has been, that is not—that is one thing. If it means there is none, that is a completely true statement" (Noah, 1998). Clinton was trying to equivocate on the word—suggesting that his affair, being in the past, was not described by a statement in the present. The representatives didn't buy it and impeached him anyway.

COUNTERING THE EQUIVOCATION

If you think someone is equivocating, ask "What do you mean by that?" or "Can you please explain that another way?" or "I hear you saying X. Is that what you mean to say?" If you are a journalist, it's important to ask for this clarification. If the source won't give it, *you* should provide it in the text. "It was not clear whether they meant. . . . They declined to clarify."

YOUR TURN

1. Clinton's impeachment trial provides still more potential Equivocation. In January 1998, speaking on television from the White House, Clinton said:

    > I want to say one thing to the American people. I want you to listen to me. I'm going to say this again. I did not have sexual relations with that woman, Ms. Lewinsky. I never told anybody

to lie. Not a single time. Never. These allegations are false. And I
need to go back to work for the American people. ("What Clinton
Said," 1998)

In fact, it was later demonstrated with DNA evidence that there
was sexual contact between Clinton and Lewinsky. What in Clinton's wording might indicate Equivocation? Given the chance, what
follow-up questions might you ask?

2. After the United States was attacked on September 11, 2001, the
Central Intelligence Agency (CIA) was interested in finding information about other planned attacks rapidly. This led to the use of what
the government called "enhanced interrogation techniques," one of
the most controversial of which was waterboarding. In waterboarding, the interrogator makes the person feel like they are drowning by
strapping them to an angled board and pouring a lot of water into
their nose and mouth. When made public, the use of this technique
was controversial, in part because it was defined as unallowable torture under some international law. The US government had its own
legal opinions issued that did not define the technique as torture.
President George W. Bush, speaking at a 2005 news conference, said

We are finding terrorists and bringing them to justice. We are gathering information about where the terrorists may be hiding. We are
trying to disrupt their plots and plans. Anything we do . . . to that
end in this effort, any activity we conduct, is within the law. We do
not torture. (Bush, "President Bush Meets with President Torrijos
of Panama," 2005)

Is Bush using Equivocation? If so, in what way? What additional
context would be needed in a news story that used that quote?

17

The Sunk Cost

"We've Already Invested so Much"

Jorge: It's icy out and not safe to drive. We should skip skiing.

Miriam: What? No! I paid a lot of money for those lift tickets for today.

DESCRIPTION OF THE ISSUE

Sometimes things are not going well and need to stop. The Sunk Cost fallacy argues that because there's already investment in a particular issue, it makes sense to keep going. If I have been paying for a gym membership and I never go, I may keep paying, with the notion that eventually I'll feel so guilty for paying all the money and start working out. This may be true; however, I may just keep paying money every month and never benefit. This is such a sure thing that it's a part of the business model for fitness facilities and other subscription businesses. Politicians and business leaders need to look like they are making decisions that pay off to keep their jobs, so sometimes they will use a Sunk Cost argument to defer change so that the consequences of bad decisions fall on someone else. They may keep manufacturing a product that isn't doing well because of the cost of setting up manufacturing, or they may keep sending troops to a losing battle because lives were already lost. Change can be hard, and sometimes even when the change might mean a choice that works better, it can be easy to convince people that taking a loss is a worse choice.

EXAMPLE

Let's say you bought a ticket to a concert six months ago and the concert is coming up in a couple of weeks. Unfortunately, you are now registered in a class that meets at night and attendance is required on the night of the concert to maintain your grade in that class. Would you decide to go to class and keep your grade up, or go to the concert because you already spent money on a ticket? Many people would go to the concert. This is an example of thinking with the Sunk Cost fallacy. You already paid for the tickets six months ago and won't get that money back. Unless the fun of the concert is more valuable to you than peace of mind about your grade, you should probably go to class.

COUNTERING THE SUNK COST FALLACY

When looking at a sunk cost, there are two factors to consider: the benefit to continue and the likely continued cost. If the cost outweighs the possible benefit, it's a bad decision to keep going. If you have a chance to ask questions, it's useful to ask what factors are going into the decision to persist and for specifics on how much has already been lost. In particular, if a strategy led to bad results in the past, what is the reason to believe it might be different in the future? Finally, it is worth considering if there is a third, lurking factor to be considered. Let's say a company buys disposable paper towels that aren't of good quality and make part of their job harder. The company decides to keep using the paper towels until they are gone, even though this choice will make the work tougher. Is the company tricking itself with the Sunk Cost fallacy? Maybe, but perhaps there is another factor like a corporate commitment to environmental sustainability that is playing a role. Before labeling an issue a problem as a Sunk Cost, consider or ask if lurking variables are in play.

YOUR TURN

1. Travel site Las Vegas Advisor ("Can you give me some tips . . . ," n.d.) suggests that a bit of strategy will help you enjoy the best value in the city's lavish buffet meal restaurants. These meals are pricey; you can pay $50 or more for a visit. So, the site assumes you want to maximize your time and the amount of food you can eat. The site suggests:

    > We know of no Las Vegas buffet that kicks out patrons between meals. Most Las Vegas buffets, however, close the cashier stations around a half-hour before the start of the new meal; as soon as

the cash registers close, the kitchen staff starts breaking down the previous meal and setting up the new one. This discourages people from taking too much advantage of the changeover.

Still, if you can get in under the breakfast or lunch wires and don't mind waiting around 20–30 minutes for lunch or dinner, it can be done. And a handful of buffets don't close between meals, so you can eat two meals for the price of one (if you leave room for the second after gorging on the first).

Wear loose-fitting or stretchy pants. You will be full afterwards; that's the whole idea!

Is this really a good strategy, or is there a Sunk Cost fallacy involved?

2.   President George W. Bush was speaking to the Veterans of Foreign Wars national convention in 2005 on a variety of topics, including the war on terror, which was a series of US military actions during his presidency that were a legacy of the attacks in New York and Washington, DC, on September 11, 2001. During the talk, he said:

> From the beaches of Normandy to the snows of Korea, courageous Americans gave their lives so others could live in freedom. Since the morning of September the 11th, we have known that the war on terror would require great sacrifice as well. We have lost 1,864 members of our Armed Forces in Operation Iraqi Freedom and 223 in Operation Enduring Freedom. Each of these men and women left grieving families and loved ones back home. Each of these heroes left a legacy that will allow generations of their fellow Americans to enjoy the blessings of liberty. And each of these Americans has brought the hope of freedom to millions who have not known it. We owe them something. We will finish the task they gave their lives for. We will honor their sacrifice by staying on the offensive against the terrorists and building strong allies in Afghanistan and Iraq that will help us win and fight—fight and win the war on terror. (Bush, "Remarks to the Veterans of Foreign Wars National Convention," 2005)

What is Bush's rationale for staying in the war? What is the risk of doing so? Is this an example of the Sunk Cost fallacy?

SECTION 2
UNRELATED EVIDENCE

◆ ◆ ◆

SOMETIMES SPEAKERS SAY THINGS that may be true but don't matter. They violate a key criterion of a good argument: that the premises relate to the conclusion (Damer, 2013, p. 113). Statements need to be evaluated for the truth, but for some speakers, that doesn't seem to be in their best interest. A much-repeated saying from the law is that when the facts are in your favor, pound the facts. When the law is in your favor, pound the law. When neither is in your favor, pound the table ("Law, facts and hostile judges," 2018). Often, sources will effectively pound the table—offering justifications for their point that have nothing to do with the facts of the matter.

A common place for this is in normative arguments, in which the speaker is trying to justify his or her opinion by considering it standard or moral. When speakers do this, the premise for accepting their point is wrapped up in some kind of a value—a virtue that they claim everyone generally agrees on. These values could be contained in a law or rule or religious precept. Constitutional values are one example. For these types of arguments to be convincing, it has to be true that the people being described as moral or normal would *actually* agree with the value. The premise is acceptable if after everyone agrees it's important, everyone can tell when it is there (it's observable), and it is supported by either logic or an authority that everyone accepts. For example, people in an organization might give moral authority to the bylaws or mission statement of that organization.

This section deals with these kinds of appeals. The listener is asked to believe based on information that may be true but is not relevant to the point the speaker is making. Your job is to find the significant information and see if that supports the point.

18

The Appeal to Pity

"If You Really Cared About Me"

Mollie: You should wash all the dishes for me.

Franklin: But it's your turn to wash them. We have an agreement.

Mollie: I know, but I'm so tired after working all day.

DESCRIPTION OF THE ISSUE

Sometimes things are legitimately bad, but that does not mean they imply a legitimately best choice. When a speaker tries to argue a point by encouraging compassion, that is an Appeal to Pity, which asks for a judgment on feelings rather than on facts. As a professor, if my student asks me to give them an excused absence for a club event they really want to attend, they are appealing to pity. They will miss out on something important to them if I do not agree. That's not a good basis of argument, because what I am actually weighing is the effect of missing what we did versus the student's ability to succeed in the class and the burden on fellow students to catch the student up or share notes. Pity isn't the important part of the decision, even if I am legitimately sympathetic. These kind of appeals are common in sentencing arguments in court, where attorneys will ask for leniency based on pity for the defendant's potential loss of opportunity, freedom or life. The Appeal to Pity is sometimes called by its Latin name, *argumentum ad misericordiam*.

EXAMPLE

Some political events easily lend themselves to an Appeal to Pity. Gun control is one because mass events of gun violence have high costs in human life and quality of life. In the 2013 State of the Union address, President Barack Obama urged gun control, saying, "The families of Oak Creek and Tucson and Blacksburg, and the countless other communities ripped open by gun violence—they deserve a simple vote" (Peralta, 2013). Gun control is a complex issue with constitutional implications, but the president was urging Congress to take up issues of gun control based on sympathy for the victims. This has the effect of allowing members who don't move bills forward to be portrayed as callous, even if their motivations are for reasons other than the victims' situations and even if they actually are sympathetic.

COUNTERING THE APPEAL TO PITY

Quotes that invoke an Appeal to Pity can be powerful, but it is your job to contextualize this for the reader. Follow-up interviews can be useful when there are differing opinions. When a speaker tries to portray an opponent as unsympathetic, in the interests of fairness, it is helpful to ask that opponent what his or her views are. This way, any false implications don't stand and the real opinion can become part of the record. In written forms, explanatory text about the history and substance of the issue is required if the information is included. It is also possible that the appeal doesn't matter to the issue being discussed and can be left out when it is explained.

YOUR TURN

1. In 1995, the US government shut down for 21 days. President Bill Clinton and a new Republican majority in the House of Representatives were at an impasse over the Republicans' desire for deep federal budget cuts and the president's desire to maintain government programs. At the time, it was the longest shutdown in history, and Clinton wanted to make sure a closure like that didn't happen again. The president gets to invite some guests to the annual State of the Union address, and he invited a federal employee. During the address, Clinton said (Clinton, 1996):

> Our federal government today is the smallest it has been in 30 years, and it's getting smaller every day. Most of our fellow Americans probably don't know that. And there is a good reason: The remaining federal work force is composed of Americans who are now working harder and working smarter than ever before, to make sure the quality of our services does not decline.

> I'd like to give you one example. His name is Richard Dean. He is a 49-year-old Vietnam veteran who's worked for the Social Security Administration for 22 years now. Last year he was hard at work in the Federal Building in Oklahoma City when the blast killed 169 people and brought the rubble down all around him. He re-entered that building four times. He saved the lives of three women. He's here with us this evening, and I want to recognize Richard and applaud both his public service and his extraordinary personal heroism.
>
> But Richard Dean's story doesn't end there. This last November, he was forced out of his office when the government shut down. And the second time the government shut down he continued helping Social Security recipients, but he was working without pay.
>
> On behalf of Richard Dean and his family, and all the other people who are out there working every day doing a good job for the American people, I challenge all of you in this Chamber: Never, ever shut the federal government down again.

Clinton was making the point that government shutdowns are hard on federal employees. Is this a good argument for negotiation with Congress? In talking about the speech, would you report the presence of Dean or share his story? If so, in how much detail?

2. In 2017, President Donald Trump fired James Comey, the director of the Federal Bureau of Investigation (FBI). The firing was interesting to Congress because the FBI was investigating the involvement of Russia in Trump's election. Some members of Congress expressed concern that the firing represented an obstruction of justice. Comey was called to testify before the Senate Select Committee on Intelligence. While he was testifying, House Majority Leader Paul Ryan addressed the press about whether the president had done anything wrong and was quoted as saying,

> The president's new at this. He's new to government, and so he probably wasn't steeped in the long-running protocols that establish the relationship between [the Justice Department], FBI and White House. He's just new to this. (Debonis, 2017)

If you were a reporter covering this press conference, would you quote this? What follow-up questions would you need to ask? What other sources of information or historical context might you provide?

19

The Appeal to Force

"Agree—or Else"

◆ ◆ ◆

Mom: You need to help me make these snacks.

Moira: I can't. I have band practice.

Mom: If you don't, I won't be finished in time for your party.

DESCRIPTION OF THE ISSUE

In the Appeal to Force, the speaker is trying to get his or her way by illustrating the bad things that will happen if not. It's a slick one because, if successful, the speaker doesn't have to present evidence that the statement is correct. The audience will go along simply because of fear of the possible consequences. For example, your friend may want to copy your work, arguing that if you don't let him or her, he or she will flunk out and you won't be able to spend time together anymore. Even if the consequences are possible or even likely, the assertion isn't proven. It's the lack of evidence that is really the problem. The Appeal to Force tries to encourage acting without enough thinking. The Appeal to Force is sometimes called by the Latin name *argumentum ad baculum*.

EXAMPLE

One hallmark of the Donald Trump presidency has been the concern over social-media company decision making and its effects on hate speech and free speech. Both sides have used an Appeal to Force to attempt to convince technology giants like Facebook, Twitter and Google to change the ways that the algorithms determine what content to share. Senator Ted Cruz said the companies could face antitrust lawsuits because they deliberately suppress conservative accounts and thoughts (Guynn, 2019). Cruz did not offer evidence of this suppression, and it is disputed. Rather than deal with the dispute, Cruz used an Appeal to Force to try to get the companies to act because of the threat of negative consequences.

COUNTERING THE APPEAL TO FORCE

When you hear an Appeal to Force, it is useful to ask for evidence that the negative consequence is necessarily going to happen. If provided, it is sometimes useful to ask why the consequence is negative, because not all of them are. For example, if tech companies are certain they would win potential antitrust lawsuits, it might not be bad if they faced one because it would clarify that they can act as they wish on those matters. If you are not able to clarify the intent with the speaker, a sentence or two of context can be helpful. Explain that the speaker didn't provide evidence for the consequence or that the consequence isn't necessarily certain. If the speaker isn't able to make the consequence happen, say so.

YOUR TURN

1. After the attacks of September 11, 2001, the United States was on edge, worried about future terrorist attacks. One concern was about Iraq. The United States had already been in a conflict with the nation several years before over Iraq's move to take over Kuwait, a US ally. Under the leadership of President George W. Bush, the federal government was concerned that Iraqi leader Saddam Hussein was developing nuclear weapons. The Bush administration was seeking allies from other countries for military action against Iraq. As Bush made the case in the United States, he spoke in October of 2002 in Ohio saying,

   > Members of Congress of both political parties, and members of the United Nations Security Council, agree that Saddam Hussein is a threat to peace and must disarm. We agree that the Iraqi dictator must not be permitted to threaten America and the world with horrible poisons and diseases and gases and atomic weapons.
   >   Since we all agree on this goal, the issue is how best can we achieve it? (Bush, 2002)

   Does Bush present evidence of the threats he describes here? Does the existence of poisons and so on mean that there is necessarily a threat to another country? Would you share this aspect of Bush's speech with a direct quotation? Why or why not?

2. The Cold War was heating up in 1961. The Union of Soviet Socialist Republics (USSR) was sitting at the top of a bloc of countries under its control and chafing at the status of Berlin, which was a city with a Western sector tucked 100 miles inside Soviet-controlled East Germany. A rash of young professionals fleeing the East for the West (19,000 in June alone) was causing tension, and the United States, the United Kingdom and France were considering how to maintain stability after World War II as the Soviets became more assertive in seeking to stop their access to parts of the city. US President John Kennedy addressed the nation in a broadcast in July of that year in "The Berlin Crisis." Kennedy wanted to reassure citizens, while also encouraging Congress to appropriate money for this developing problem so that the armed forces could be of help to the people of Berlin. Kennedy said:

> If new threats in Berlin or elsewhere should cause us to weaken our program of assistance to the developing nations who are also under heavy pressure from the same source, or to halt our efforts for realistic disarmament, or to disrupt or slow down our economy, or to neglect the education of our children, then those threats will surely be the most successful and least costly manoeuvre in Communist history. For we can afford all these efforts, and more, but we cannot afford not to meet this challenge. (Kennedy, 1961)

What is the logic Kennedy was using? Does he provide evidence for, or details about, the threats he is describing? What follow-up questions might you ask to contextualize Kennedy's words?

20

The Appeal to Ignorance

"No One Has Proved You Can't"

Francis: Professor Foster must be great.

Carl: How do you know?

Francis: There's no bad stuff on Rate My Professor.

DESCRIPTION OF THE ISSUE

If you can't disprove something, that doesn't necessarily mean it is true. In the Appeal to Ignorance, the issue may be a lack of evidence or a weakness in the way it could be proven, for example if evidence exists, but you can't access it. I might tell my friends they can be sure my children are happy that I make them clean up the kitchen after dinner every night because I haven't heard any complaining. My lack of knowledge doesn't make it true, though. It's possible that they have been complaining on Snapchat to their friends, but because I can't access that evidence, I don't know how they feel. Speakers will use this strategy when they try to fault their opponents for not providing evidence. The Appeal to Ignorance is sometimes called by its Latin name, *argumentum ad ignorantium*.

EXAMPLE

Cavender and Kahane (2006) give the example from the 1950s of Senator Joseph McCarthy who was asked about a person he asserted was connected to communism and working for the US State Department. He replied, "I do not have much information on this except the general statement of the agency that there is nothing in the files to disprove his communist connections" (p. 83). Failure of the negative is not the same as the positive; lack of information in the file doesn't prove that the staff member was a communist.

COUNTERING THE APPEAL TO IGNORANCE

It is difficult to prove a complete absence, so you may be able to find a counterexample to include in your story. This doesn't have to come from your own setting. A lawmaker who wants a tax cut might say that there is no evidence that lowering taxes increases budget deficits because your town has cut taxes a few times and each time, deficits did not rise. You might be able to use the experience of other similar cities that had a different experience to frame a question about why your city is different. If the risk is hypothetical, you can just state that in the story, providing evidence. "Although tax cuts have not increased deficits in Springfield's history, Springfield University economics professor Leon Spinney said the city budget may be too slim to support one." Or, you can simply say that "although isn't hasn't happened yet, this doesn't mean it's impossible in the future."

YOUR TURN

1. In 2012, North Carolina voters approved an amendment to the state constitution that prohibited the state from recognizing gay marriages and other civil unions. In the run-up to the vote, North Carolina State Representative Paul Stam, the majority leader, spoke as part of a public debate on the proposal. Stam (2012) said, "I calculated on the back of an envelope that since that time there have been about twenty-five thousand bills filed. Of those twenty-five thousand bills that have been filed by your predecessors (and maybe yourselves) not a single one of them has attempted to change the policy that we have about marriage." The year 1996 was important because the state had passed a law banning same-sex marriage, with a large majority of the legislature in support. Stam is arguing that because no one filed a bill to change the 1996 law, people must agree with it.

    In what sense could this be an Appeal to Ignorance? How would you handle this in a story?

2. When Michael Dukakis, the governor of Massachusetts, was running against George H. W. Bush in 1988 for president, one element of persuasion was about the patriotism of each candidate. Bush said that Dukakis was a "card-carrying member of the ACLU." Dukakis accused Bush of lacking patriotism by saying the following:

The fact of the matter is that if the Pledge of Allegiance was the acid test of one's patriotism—the Vice President's been the presiding officer in the United States Senate for the past seven and a half years—to the best of my knowledge he's never once suggested that a session of the Senate begin with the Pledge of Allegiance. ("Transcript of first TV debate" 1988)

Is this sufficient evidence to prove Bush's patriotism or lack of same? If not, what is lacking? What context could you include in writing a piece about this part of the debate?

21

The Appeal to Authority

"I'm Not a Doctor, But . . ."

◆ ◆ ◆

Salma: Oh, no, I have a brain tumor.

Pete: That's terrible! What did the doctor say?

Salma: Oh, I haven't talked to a doctor. But I searched for "headache" online and that was the first result.

DESCRIPTION OF THE ISSUE

Journalists use expert sources all the time to provide qualified opinion on issues, and they are trained to assess the qualifications of experts. But they can still have problems when they are using sources who claim they are relying on expert opinion, but they aren't really. The Appeal to Authority is when something is assumed to be true because an expert said it. There are three ways to get in trouble with this. The first is when the cited authority is referenced but not named. Whenever sources refer to a report, commission or group as supporting their idea, you need to know which one they used. The second is when the authority is biased or otherwise suspect. The third is when the group or person cited is an authority but not in the domain being cited. In each of these cases, it is up to you to evaluate the credibility of the authority on matters such as training, experience and bias. Don't just take the source's use as proof. The Appeal to Authority is sometimes called by its Latin name, *argumentum ad vericundiam.*

EXAMPLE

Beginning in the 1970s, some people began taking large doses of vitamin C in hopes of preventing colds. They were following the advice of Dr.

Linus Pauling, a scientist who won the Nobel Prize in chemistry, which is an impressive qualification that few have obtained. (In fact, Pauling is one of only four people ever to hold multiple Nobel Prizes; he also won the Nobel Peace Prize). Chemistry is not medicine, however. There have been scientific battles over the belief in vitamin C, and some well-designed trials have found little evidence to date that vitamin C actually prevents colds. In fact, the amount of vitamin C Pauling recommended, 2,000 mg per day, is actually greater than the amount the National Institutes of Health (NIH) states the human body can absorb. Although research in nutrition and medicine continues to move forward, basing a daily dose of vitamin C on the authority of Dr. Pauling would be misguided because although he was an accomplished scientist, he doesn't have expertise related to this question.

COUNTERING THE APPEAL TO AUTHORITY

Before you quote someone, you need to know not only your sources, but also your sources' sources as you assess credibility. It is fair to your readers to identify those sources in text and to also provide context to help audiences draw their own conclusions about credibility. If a politician says, "A poll in my state shows everyone supports me," a follow-up statement might be, "The candidate was referring to the WKWW-TV Twitter poll. Twitter polls are not scientific." Note that you need to be aware of the possibility that someone without formal credentials may still have relevant knowledge. For example, a day care worker may not have a degree in child development, but many years of direct experience with children may allow that worker to have expertise in some aspects of child behavior or even development. Questions about context for this kind of authority are especially important; your audience will need to know quite a bit about the worker's experiences to make decisions about the source's credibility.

YOUR TURN

1. The case of Terry Schaivo was a right-to-die case in Florida in 2005. Schaivo suffered a heart attack in 1990 and was without oxygen for enough time that she become unresponsive; two different neurologists diagnosed her as being in a "persistent vegetative state," meaning there was not a chance that she would improve. She was able to breathe and her heart beat independently, but she needed nutrition from a feeding tube to survive. In 1998, her husband, Michael, petitioned the state to allow her feeding tube to be removed. She did not

have a document indicating her preferences, but a court trial determined that she had made statements that she would not want to be kept alive indefinitely. Terry's parents fought the motion in court, and federal government officials, including President George W. Bush and several members of Congress, became involved. Senator Bill Frist, a Republican from Tennessee, gave an impassioned speech on the matter, supporting Terry's parents.

> Persistent vegetative state, which is what the court has ruled—I say that I question it. I question it based on a review of the video footage which I spent an hour or so looking at last night in my office here in the capitol. And that footage, to me, depicts something very different than persistent vegetative state. (Hook, 2005)

Frist, a transplant surgeon, then quoted from an internal medicine textbook as evidence that Schaivo didn't meet the definition of that state. Given that determinations of vegetative state are made by neurologists on the basis of examining patients, how would you handle Frist's remarks, on the record on the floor of the Senate, in a story?

2. In 2019, Texas congressional representative Matthew Schaefer tweeted a series of position statements about laws relating to guns in the United States, including the following:

> I am NOT going to use the evil acts of a handful of people to diminish the God-given rights of my fellow Texans. Period. None of these so-called gun-control solutions will work to stop a person with evil intent.

In a series of responses, actress and activist Alyssa Milano replied, also on Twitter:

> Can someone cite which passage of the Bible God states it is a god-given right to own a gun? This guy is unbelievable and is clearly owned by the gun lobby.

US Senator Ted Cruz, also from Texas, responded:

> An excellent Q, worth considering carefully w/o the snark of Twitter. It is of course not the right to a modern-day firearm that is God-give but rather the right to Life & the right to Liberty. Essential to that right to life is the right to DEFEND your life & your family. (Scott, 2019)

Cruz continued with a quote of Exodus 22:2:

> If a thief is caught breaking in at night & is struck a fatal blow, the defender is not guilty of bloodshed.

Why is Milano questioning Schaefer? To what authority is Schaefer attributing the right to possess arms? Does Cruz's reply answer the authority question? Does it answer Milano's question?

22

The Appeal to Tradition

"We've Always Done It This Way"

Chandler: I can't wait to play in the Powderpuff Football Game for girls.

Aisha: Really? Don't a lot of girls get hurt doing that?

Chandler: I guess. But it's an East High favorite. Even my Mom played in it.

DESCRIPTION OF THE ISSUE

Tradition can be a good thing that helps keep a community together, but traditions are not always the best practices as societies evolve and change. In one form of the Appeal to Tradition, the speaker may state that something should happen in a particular way because that's the way it has been for years. Whether it's putting a turkey on the Thanksgiving table or what music to have at a wedding, tradition can cause disagreements in families. But knowledge moves on and societies change. Sometimes, following tradition isn't the best idea. For example, older generations thought it was a good idea to put butter on a burn, a practice we now know increases the likelihood of infection. Particularly when it comes to social issues, speakers will sometimes use tradition as a rationale for how things should be done. When tradition is the only reason, the merits of the practice aren't discussed.

A second sense is when the speaker is referring to an abstract idea that should then guide action. This is a particularly messy issue when most people in a society will at least say they agree with that ideal. For example, if Americans agree that the structure of government laid down in the Constitution of the United States is a functional, or even superior

76

structure of government, people who consider changes face accusations of going against the ideals laid down by the Founding Fathers. This leads to a debate on the opposition's loyalty rather than to the merits of the issue. The Appeal to Tradition is sometimes called by a Latin name, *argumentum ad antiquitatem*.

EXAMPLE

The notion of "mom wisdom" is so strong that there are memes and sketch comedy bits about it, and the Appeal to Tradition is a central feature. But sometimes that traditional wisdom ends up doing harm. One case is Sudden Infant Death Syndrome (SIDS). For many years, doctors advised, and mothers believed, that it was best to put babies to sleep on their stomachs because the babies would sleep better (and the moms and dads would get more rest). Later study showed that this was a bad idea because it put babies at risk of getting stuck in a position and suffocating. Visiting grandmothers still encourage tired moms to put their babies down on their stomachs. Occasionally, there will also be a funny list that circulates on social media saying that the current generation survived riding without seatbelts, drinking out of the hose outside and so on and did just fine. These traditional childhood activities must not be harmful, the logic goes. But the ones who read and snicker at the list are the ones who weren't harmed and did survive. Just because something is traditional doesn't mean it's the best. The merits need evidence and testing.

COUNTERING THE APPEAL TO TRADITION

There are a few ways to handle the Appeal to Tradition. If there is evidence that the tradition isn't best practice, you can provide that evidence and ask the speaker what he or she makes of it. In the example in Your Turn, you might ask managers you interview about what they gain from keeping workers together that is more valuable than what they spend on keeping maintaining office space. Another thing to consider is if the traditional practice or opinion is, in fact, traditional. For example, in US Pledge of Allegiance has a line "One nation, under God," and this line has been used as a justification for arguments about religious liberty practices. Noting that the line was added to the pledge in the 1950s, you could ask the speaker to react to that, or use it yourself in a story to provide the context that the purportedly traditional isn't much of a tradition in this case because the pledge dates to the 1890s, with the phrase added much later.

YOUR TURN

1. Rick Santorum ran for the Republican nomination for president twice, and, trying to distinguish himself from other candidates, he presented himself as a candidate strongly informed by his Christian faith. In a CBS interview, he addressed his belief that a Supreme Court ruling effectively needed to be overturned. He said that although his opponents saw the court's ruling as settling the matter,

> What we know is best from thousands of years of human history is for children to be raised with mothers and fathers, preferably but not always their biological mothers and fathers. Adoptive homes are great and wonderful places too.
>
> We have laws that say, "Fathers, really you don't have to raise your children; mothers, you know, we're going to provide all sorts of things that make fathers less necessary."
>
> We have now said marriage is not about having children, so people are not getting married. That's not a good situation to maximize the potential for each and every one of our children. And that's what I'm really talking about here. (Pengelly, 2015)

   On what basis is Santorum arguing that heterosexual marriage is better? Is he providing evidence? If so, is that evidence sufficient? If you were including this quotation in a story, what additional context would you provide?

2. Usually, a company's office workers will travel each day to work together in the same space. This has a lot of associated costs, including rising early, buying workplace clothing, transportation and hours of child care for children of employees. It has costs for the business as well, as it maintains office space and other facilities like bathrooms that have enough capacity to support all the workers at the same time. Those same facilities usually sit empty for half the hours in a day, while the company pays for utilities and someone to clean the space. New technology has made it possible for coworkers to keep in constant contact and move files with ease. Not only that, research shows that many employees prefer to work from home, and even when they are in the same office, they still communicate primarily over the same technology that they would use to work from home. There are also social benefits to teleworking like less traffic and less pollution. Yet, many employees would like to work from home but are told they can't because it's not a traditional model for an office. In 2013, Yahoo! CEO Marisa Mayer distressed employees by telling

them that the company's policies allowing work from home were going away. The company's head of human resources, Jackie Reses, wrote a memo that said:

> To become the absolute best place to work, communication and collaboration will be important, so we need to be working side-by-side. That is why it is critical that we are all present in our offices. . . . Speed and quality are often sacrificed when we work from home. We need to be one Yahoo, and that starts with physically being together. (Cited in Thompson, 2013)

This quote doesn't mention tradition. Is it still an Appeal to Tradition? What are the manager's claims? Does she offer evidence? What evidence might you ask her to provide if you were writing a news piece about the move?

23

The Appeal to Popularity

"A Lot of People Agree"

◆ ◆ ◆

Ronald: That store must have really good merchandise.

Luke: Why would you say that?

Ronald: See how many people are in there?

DESCRIPTION OF THE ISSUE

When a speaker says something is good because a lot of people like it, this is an Appeal to Popularity. From the sign at McDonald's restaurants stating how many people have been served to the wait for tickets for the hot, new show to the number of stars in an online review, popularity is an easy shorthand for value. It's also a risky one. Sometimes you get lucky and the crowd is correct. Sometimes you don't, and the evidence suggests otherwise. An Appeal to Popularity can quickly fall apart in the face of evidence that the crowd is wrong. YouTube personality Danny Gonzalez is one of many comedians who make a career of mocking popular videos and other pieces of culture, showing that the ideas in the video don't make sense or don't work. Appeal to Popularity is common in advertising and in politics. In advertising, messages may rely on the bandwagon effect—suggesting that everyone wants to "be a Pepper" by drinking Dr Pepper or that you'd be happy with a Timex watch because it is the "choice of millions." Politicians will sometimes present themselves as the stronger candidate by virtue of doing what people want, rather than talking about the best solutions. The Appeal to Popularity is sometimes called by the Latin name *argumentum ad populum*.

EXAMPLE

President Jimmy Carter was speaking in 1978 to commemorate the 30th anniversary of the Universal Declaration of Human Rights at the White House. He said:

> The American people want the actions of their government, both to reduce human suffering and to increase human freedom. That's why— with the help and encouragement of many of you in this room—I have sought to rekindle the beacon of human rights in American foreign policy. (Carter, 1978, p. 2162)

Carter is saying he is doing the will of those who elected him, which is usually a hallmark of responsive governance. However, you could also see the words he uses to justify actions as an Appeal to Popularity. He goes on to list policy initiatives that stem from this appeal, including instructing US envoys to give clear messages about preserving freedom, fighting bigotry and allocating foreign aid to countries who support democracy. Even though democracy and human rights seem like good things, it's not correct to assume that everyone believes they are the only ones that matter in decision making. For example, economic development can be seen as a short-term cost for a long-term benefit. If 10 people have to give up their homes and move so that 100 people can be employed in a factory on that same land, you could argue that, that would be a greater good and the better course of action.

COUNTERING THE APPEAL TO POPULARITY

You may have tried an Appeal to Popularity on your Mom when you told her everyone had a phone or a car or everyone's parents let them hang out in a parking lot on Friday nights. She may have countered something like. "If everyone's parents were letting them jump off a cliff, should I let you do it?" Snappy answers aside, a simple question can help you get beyond the Appeal to Popularity. "What's your evidence that this thing works?" If the answer is a repeat of the popularity argument, you can provide a counterexample in which the crowd was wrong. For example, some Internet-fueled popular fads turn out to be dangerous, like the planking fad, where people would post pictures of themselves lying stiff in places, and an Australian man fell off his roof doing so (Castillo, 2011).

YOUR TURN

1. Vermont senator and sometimes presidential candidate Bernie Sanders has been an outspoken advocate of universal health care. He has given evidence-based arguments but not consistently. For example, in a 2015 interview, he said, "We need to join the rest of the industrialized world. We are the only major country on Earth that doesn't guarantee health care to all people as a right" (Greenberg, 2015). Here, Sanders is appealing to a popular idea in other places to suggest that it's right for the United States as well. Is this sufficient evidence that the United States should guarantee health care? What pieces of the argument are missing? What questions would you ask?

2. In 1969, President Richard Nixon was facing vocal opposition to the protracted and bloody conflict in Vietnam. Nixon had campaigned on a plan to end the war, but after election, he sought to reduce the US presence but continue the fight. This policy brought protests and other backlash, and Nixon addressed the country on November 3, 1969, saying:

> I recognize that some of my fellow citizens disagree with the plan for peace that I have chosen. Honest and patriotic Americans have reached different conclusions as to how peace should be achieved. In San Francisco a few weeks ago, I saw demonstrators carrying signs reading, "Lose the war in Vietnam. Bring the boys home."
>
> Well, one of the strengths of our society is that any American has a right to reach that conclusion and to advocate that point of view. But as President of the United States, I would be untrue to my oath of office to be dictated by the minority who hold that point of view and who try to impose it on the nation by mounting demonstrations in the street. . . . Let historians not record that, when America was the most powerful nation in the world, we passed on the other side of the road and allowed the last hopes for peace and freedom of millions of people to be suffocated by the forces of totalitarianism. So tonight, to you, the great silent majority of my fellow Americans, I ask for your support. (Nixon, 1969)

What is Nixon's evidence for the support for continuing the war? What is the role of the "silent majority" in his support? What clarifications might you seek about the silent majority to contextualize a story?

24

The Big Lie and Conspiracy Theories

"The Sky Is Green. The Sky Is Green. The Sky Is Green"

John: I'm really smart.

Mary: You graduated with a D average.

John: I'm really smart.

Mary: You can't figure out how much paint you need for a room, even with a calculator.

John: I'm a genius.

Mary: Maybe you are smarter than you seem.

DESCRIPTION OF THE ISSUE

The Big Lie is a propaganda technique in which the speaker says something untrue—but wildly so. People who are confident of their ability to think independently are especially susceptible to this propaganda technique, which depends on people's bias for wanting to believe that things are true. Adolf Hitler wrote about the Big Lie in *Mein Kampf*, stating that the technique works because the listener can't accept that the speaker would have any incentive to create such "colossal untruths" (Hitler, 2014). To produce the big lie, speakers must know that the information is untrue, yet say it with conviction, repeating it and, if needed, bringing in misinterpreted "evidence" in support of the lie. They will never back down and will call those who try to disprove them bad actors who are trying to hide the truth. The Big Lie can be the basis of Conspiracy Theories, in which believers hold tightly to convincingly delivered, repeated assertions even in the face of little evidence. The results for society can be catastrophic.

EXAMPLE

Comet Ping Pong is a pizzeria in Washington, DC. The restaurant on Connecticut Avenue does not have a basement, but a fictitious Big Lie led to a real shooting at the restaurant and, later, an attempted arson. A Twitter account initially stated that the restaurant was a locus for a child sex-trafficking operation in the restaurant's basement that was linked to an underground network for crime. Initial proponents claimed that secret clues in the text of leaked e-mails published by Wikileaks were proof of Democratic involvement in the alleged scheme. The lie was posted on pro-Trump websites and spread by alt-right personalities and others on social media, eventually being taken up by bots from several other countries and media in Turkey. Shortly after the 2016 election, a North Carolina man drove to DC and fired shots in the pizzeria in an attempt to help the children he believed were being abused there (Haag and Salam, 2017). Although there were media outlets that published pieces debunking the rumor, the strength of the lie was such that even in 2019, someone started a fire at the restaurant after leaving a diaper and some baby food (Hernandez, 2019).

COUNTERING THE BIG LIE

It is difficult to ask a source to justify a Big Lie during an interview, and particularly in a broadcast setting, it can be unwise because it can degenerate into a journalist asking the same question while the source repeats the lie. This can have the effect of spreading misinformation, even if that is not the journalist's intent. Correct information with the source identified can be included in the context portions of a story or package, if it is vital to include the source's misinformation to identify a cause. For example, you might write, "Welch, the North Carolina man convicted of discharging a weapon in the pizzeria, told police he believed the restaurant was part of a child sex ring. Numerous media outlets have debunked this claim, demonstrating that there is no child sex ring affiliated with the restaurant." If the Big Lie is not about a matter in the current public interest, consider carefully if it is worth covering at all.

YOUR TURN

1. In the 2018 elections, Democrats Andrew Gillum and Stacey Abrams narrowly lost gubernatorial elections in Florida and Georgia, respectively. In both states, there were changes to voter rolls that some felt ultimately affected the outcome. Regardless, Gillum and Abrams did lose. But senator and then presidential candidate Kamala Harris repeated in speeches and social media the idea that they should have won. She said. "Let's say this loud and clear—without voter suppression, Stacey Abrams would be the governor of Georgia, Andrew Gillum is the governor of Florida" (Hutzler, 2019). Is this true? If it is not clear, write a few sentences you might include in a story or script to contextualize the remarks.

2. When HIV/AIDS was first identified as an issue, it was known to be transmitted by homosexual sex. It did spread among heterosexuals as well, with high rates of transmission persisting among Black people. There were quite a few rumors about the origin of the disease, including an international disinformation campaign that claimed that the United States had created the disease in a lab to spread to other countries as a type of biological weapon against Africans and African Americans (US Department of State, 1987). In 1992, actor/director Spike Lee was quoted in an ad for clothing line Benetton as saying:

   I'm convinced AIDS is a government-engineered disease. They got one thing wrong; they never realized it couldn't just be contained to the groups it was intended to wipe out. So now it's a national priority. Exactly like drugs become when they escaped the urban centers into White suburbia. (Cited in Heller, 2015)

   Is it responsible to repeat this quote? In what context? Would you repeat it as a controversial claim? Would you try to provide context?

SECTION 3
ISSUES WITH NUMBERS AND DATA

◆ ◆ ◆

NUMERACY REFERS TO SOMEONE'S ABILITY to understand numbers and what they mean. Even people who were good at math in school can be innumerate. This represents a real issue for deception for two reasons. First, people who report and share information can be confused by numbers. If the reporter doesn't understand what is being said, he or she is not likely to explain it clearly. Second, even if the information is shared correctly, the audience may be innumerate and may interpret the meaning incorrectly. In either case, it can be easy to deceive by using numbers.

Being able to do the operations of math like integration or division of fractions is not the same as really understanding the meaning behind the mathematics. People who communicate with and about numbers must first understand what the numbers actually mean. If a writer or editor feels at all uncertain, it is appropriate to go to an expert for confirmation, like with any fact that's in doubt. For their part, spokespeople need to make sure they understand what the numbers mean and that they communicate clearly.

This section covers some common issues in numeracy, both in understanding issues like polls and surveys and in reporting with numbers. When sharing news about numbers, think about the ways the audience could misinterpret them and make sure to be clear about what is being reported. Stories about numbers should always have context for what the numbers mean.

25

Ignoring the Base Rate

"100 Percent of People Die"

Haman: I'm so proud of my daughter. She finished third in her high school class.

Jolene: But wait, there are only three kids in her school.

DESCRIPTION OF THE ISSUE

When you are looking at placement, change or improvement, there is always a context. Removing a claim from its context can be deceptive. If a story about a city's residents with HIV/AIDS said that 80 percent of men younger than age 35 in the city died every year as a result of the disease, this would seem terrible. This is a huge epidemic and may require quarantining the city, if true. But the reporter made the mistake of ignoring the base rate. Men younger than age 34 are unlikely to die for any reason—the average death rate nationwide for that group was less than 1 percent in 2016. If the 80 percent is of *men who die*, that's a different thing and is not ignoring the base rate. Sometimes people deliberately misuse the base rate to be deceptive.

If a town wants to claim that it has lowered crime rates, the town's public relations (PR) spokesperson might throw out statistics like a 50-percent reduction in homicides in the last year. A candidate in the same town might want to argue that the city is dangerous and needs to elect her to "clean up crime." How can this be the same place? The PR spokesperson might be thinking, "Two years ago, there were four homicides. This year there were two, so that's a 50 percent improvement." Out of a base rate of four, that *is* a good improvement. On the other hand the candidate might be thinking, "We're a town of 50—losing even one person is too many." The context really matters.

89

You can also see examples of this in people's views of the world around them. People tend to surround themselves with like-minded people when they can; it's easier to not have to argue all the time, for one thing. Social-media site algorithms do this as well by putting content you are likely to enjoy (agree with) at the top of your feed. Over time, it's easy to get a misperception that everyone thinks the way that you do. But even if many students at a particular college feel a particular way, that doesn't mean that they all do. And even if many people in a particular neighborhood or town feel the same way, that doesn't mean that all people in the state or the country do. A good example of this is Twitter, which is a more niche social-media site. If you base your views on what is popular in your country or city based on what trends there on Twitter, you are going to misinterpret the facts because you are just looking a slice of the bigger picture. Ignoring the Base Rate is related to errors in understanding polls and surveys and to Hasty Generalizations.

EXAMPLES

In 2018, Attorney General Jeff Sessions gave a speech at a Department of Justice Religious Liberty Summit. He made the assertion that religious liberty was under attack in the United States: "the cultural climate in this country—and in the West more generally—has become less hospitable to people of faith. Many Americans have felt that their freedom to practice their faith has been under attack." The first piece of evidence that he gave was, "We've seen nuns ordered to buy contraceptives," (Sessions, 2018). Sessions was referring to a prominent legal case in which the Little Sisters of the Poor sought an exception to a requirement to refer people on their health insurance plan to places where covered people might secure contraceptive coverage. Specifics of that case aside, "many" is an unclear reference that could represent Ignoring the Base Rate. About 20 percent of Americans identify as Catholic, and up to two-thirds of those told researchers they wanted the church to allow birth control. It's not all Americans, or even all Catholics, that are being considered. Sessions is making an argument that sounds like it relates to all people of faith but using an example that is a much smaller number of people.

A famous case of this was in the trial of O.J. Simpson, a successful football player and later actor who was accused of a double murder—of killing both his wife and her friend. Attorney Alan Dershowitz helped advise Simpson's legal team. One of the issues during the trial was that there was evidence that Simpson had beaten his wife, and he had even been arrested for it. Wouldn't it make sense that a person who injured someone else in the past might kill them in the future? During the trial, Dershowitz publicly stated that he didn't think that mattered because only one-tenth of a percent of spouse abusers go on to kill their spouses (Cummins and Allen, 1998, p. 18). Therefore, attorneys implied, because Simpson had been arrested for battering his wife, he was extremely unlikely to have killed her. Interviews with people on the jury suggested that an argument like this worked for some because they didn't see the relationship of beating and murder as being relevant. It is relevant, but the base rate should be people who are murdered and not just people who are murdered by their spouses. Looking at it that way, it's definitely worth considering if an abused victim was killed by their abuser because there's a 50/50 chance (Cummins and Allen, 1998, p. 19). This kind of misunderstanding of the base rate can have real-world consequences. Simpson was exonerated in his criminal trial for the murder but was later convicted of wrongful death for the same crime in a civil case brought by the family of Ronald Goldman, Nicole Simpson's friend who died in the same incident.

COUNTERING THE IGNORING THE BASE RATE

Numbers stories must always include context. Whenever you see a statistic or figure, you need to ask the newsmaker or otherwise find "out of what" or "compared to what" the numbers presented refer to. This context needs to be included in your story so your readers can judge the importance of the information. A school district press release might state the following:

> "This year's SAT scores went up for the third year in a row," the superintendent said. "Overall scores have gone up five points over three years."

Knowing, as you do, that the SAT is scored out of 1600 points, you'd have to wonder if this press release is worth a story at all. Perhaps this information could be part of a larger piece on "how the schools are doing" that used a variety of metrics, though. If you ran that, you'd want to ask some follow-up questions like if that was overall score, if that was for all test-takers or a subgroup like juniors and also to ask what percentage of students in the school take the SAT, because in some locations the ACT is the more popular test. Then, in the story, you need to provide context about the base rate for the readers. You could say, "The SAT is scored with 1600 available points," so that the audience knows that a 5-point change doesn't really mean much. Consider carefully whether reporting the numbers of base rate and statistic or percentage of change will make more sense to the reader.

YOUR TURN

A *New York Times* magazine article by Andrew Ross Sorkin (Sorkin, 2018) suggested that banks should combine and share information on gun purchases to catch people planning terrorist attacks. Sorkin used the example of Omar Mateen, who bought two guns and thousands of rounds of ammunition before killing 49 people and injuring 53 others at the Pulse Nightclub in Orlando, Florida, in 2016. Sorkin also used as evidence credit card records from other mass shooters, including in Las Vegas and Aurora, Colorado, to suggest that the financial system should flag purchases of guns and large amounts of ammunition to forward to law enforcement for follow-up. Is this a good idea for public safety or a violation of civil liberties? These are big questions, but one that's more straightforward to consider is whether Sorkin's proposal represents a misinterpretation of the base rate. Does it? If so, how might you clarify the assumptions being made clearly in the story?

26

The False Cause

"Spider Bites and Spelling Bees"

Monique: I was watching this TV show about ghost hunting, and it was weird because the lights in my house kept dimming.

Ole: You must have made the spirits mad.

DESCRIPTION OF THE ISSUE

When things are related in time and space, it can be tempting to assume that the events are related, and this can be wrong because of a False Cause. Sometimes things change at the same time, but it's not because they are actually related in any meaningful way. Tyler Vigen (2015) maintains a gallery of false correlations, including things like the amount of cheese consumed is highly related to the number of accidental strangulations and suffocations in bed and Nicolas Cage film roles in a year correlate with drowning deaths (Vigen, 2015, p. 1). Just because things happen at the same time doesn't mean one causes the other. A False Cause is when someone claims that one thing caused the other, when one did not actually bring the other about.

EXAMPLE

When people have chemotherapy, the medicines used tend to have severe nausea as a side effect. This can be a problem because people will sometimes become repulsed by foods they eat right before they become ill with a stomach issue. This is called *food aversion* and would usually be a good thing—if you are eating something that makes you sick, you would want your body to help you remember to not eat that thing again. For patients with cancer, though, it can be a real problem because they develop an aversion to the food they ate right before the chemotherapy for no good reason. Their body falsely assumes that the food made them sick, which is a False Cause. An interesting study (Mattes, 1994) suggested that deliberately giving a patient with cancer a food they don't normally eat as the last thing before chemotherapy may cause them to attribute the nausea to that food instead.

COUNTERING THE FALSE CAUSE

Correlations, positive or negative, require that one thing be before the other and that things consistently vary together. Cause requires that the cause is first thing is essential for the second to happen. The best correlations last over time and are tested with controls that can show that other explanations aren't what's causing the effect (see chapter 27). You should ask newsmakers how and over what time period the correlation was observed. You should also check other sources to see if something else could explain the relationship. Ask the newsmaker why those factors aren't the determining ones.

Advertisements often have implied causes like that drinking certain carbonated beverages will make you popular. It is important to think critically about the source of the claim and the real meaning of the claim. Finally, whenever you can observe original data, you should to draw your own conclusions.

In other cases, it might be that the relationship is reversed, confusing the cause for the effect. If you notice that at the same time the temperature goes below 32 degrees Farenheit, puddles begin to freeze, it would be possible to conclude when water freezes, it makes the temperature go down. We know that this is wrong. Politicians will frequently use this kind of thinking to blame present situations on things that happened while a predecessor was in office, without offering evidence that it was the predecessor's fault. For example, Hillary Clinton argued that tax cuts under George W. Bush were the cause of a substantial 2009 recession. Kessler (2016) notes that though the tax cuts preceded the recession, there isn't good evidences that the tax cuts were the cause. Sometimes, people will also take credit for things that happened when they were in power that they, themselves, did not cause.

YOUR TURN

1. People think that college is a way to get a leg up in life, so this quote from the *Chronicle of Higher Education* might have been a real surprise.

If you want a life full of sexual pleasures, don't go to graduate school. In fact, don't even graduate from college. A study to be published next month in American Demographics magazine shows that people with the most education have the least amount of sex. ("Study Finds More Educated People . . . ," 1998).

What is the implied effect of a college education? Identify if there is evidence within or outside the passage to support that relationship. If there is not, write the context you would include in your story or package to make the relationship clear.

2. President Donald Trump spoke and tweeted often about economic growth that occurred during his presidency. In particular, he mentioned the improvement in unemployment, tweeting on December 23, 2017, "The Stock Market is setting record after record and unemployment is at a 17 year low. So many things accomplished by the Trump Administration, perhaps more than any other President in first year. Sadly, will never be reported correctly by the Fake News Media!" (Rampell, 2019). Here is the data from the Bureau of Labor Statistics of unemployment each December since President Obama was in office: 2009 (9.7); 2010 (9.1); 2011 (8.3); 2012 (7.6); 2013 (6.5); 2014 (5.4); 2015 (4.8); 2016 (4.5); 2017 (3.9). The unemployment rate was low and did go down since the last year of the Obama presidency. Is there evidence that the Trump administration is the cause? If you were writing a story about this claim, what questions would you need to ask to contextualize the information?

27

The Hidden Variable

"Rabbit Feet and Lucky Rocks"

◆ ◆ ◆

Violet: This dessert tastes terrible.

Claude: I followed the recipe exactly.

Violet: Wait, is that salt in the sugar container?

DESCRIPTION OF THE ISSUE

The Hidden Variable is related to False Cause in that you have two things that appear to be causally related, but they are not proven to be. In this case, though, there is a third, uncredited factor that causes the change. A common example is the relationship of ice cream sales and bicycle theft. The careful observer might note that every year, both increase at the same time. So which is it? Are bicycle thieves partial to ice cream? Or does eating ice cream make you crave two-wheeled transportation? Of course, neither explanation makes sense. The warmer summer weather makes frozen treats appealing and encourages bicycle riding, which means more bicycles are out and available to steal. Summer weather is the lurking variable.

EXAMPLES

A teacher might look at her class of children and notice that the taller students seem to be the better scholars: They pay attention better and have learned to read better, too. She thinks to herself that height must be related to intelligence. This ignores an important Hidden Variable: age. Children tend to grow taller as they age. Older children tend to have more ability to control their attention spans, which, in turn, helps in gaining academic skill.

Here's another example. Some people will fail to get the flu shot because they think the shot causes the flu, but it's not biologically possible. Some people will get the shot and develop symptoms like a runny nose and cough right after. Flu shots are advised by the end of October in the United States, which is the same time that the weather gets colder and more people spend time in close quarters indoors, which is a good candidate for a Hidden Variable. It's also the time when children go back to school, meaning they are close together for many hours a day. Colds can have some symptoms that are like the flu, and it's likely that close contact could be a reason people develop similar symptoms from an unrelated disease soon after a flu shot—another chance for a Hidden Variable.

COUNTERING THE HIDDEN VARIABLE

Consider and ask about other possible explanations. Your own sense of context and history can be helpful in identifying possible competing explanations, and you should consider this when you are interviewing people reporting the results of experts. Going back to the source to check an interpretation can also be helpful. For example, if a politician offers an explanation for decreasing unemployment based on data from the Bureau of Labor Statistics, a call to a spokesperson at the bureau can help save you from including a misleading quote in your story.

YOUR TURN

1. Godoy (2013) writes about the case of Kellogg's Frosted Mini-Wheats cereal, which said in an advertisement that research showed that children who ate the cereal "improved their attentiveness by nearly 20 percent." Before you used this statistic or repeated it, what kinds of things would you need to know about the study? What might be a potential Hidden Variable?

2. British tabloid newspapers created quite a stir with stories about a series of home fires that had a mysterious commonality—many of the homes had a particular painting of a crying boy hung up in the house, and in some cases, that painting was the only possession that the homeowners had that survived the fire. Stories sprang up about the painting's ability to survive fire as well as more mythical

tales about the painting even being able to start fires. The story ran in *The Sun* in the United Kingdom (UK) in 1985 (Cited in Zarrelli, 2017), and the incident has been reused in Halloween roundups of spooky happenings in the UK as well as in newspapers in other countries in the British Commonwealth more than two decades later. The painting was mass produced and sold in department stores as a sort of generic home art and was a popular adornment in working-class homes since. If you were running a spooky roundup story today, what Hidden Variable could you identify that might explain the association between owning the painting and having your house burn down? Why might the painting survive fires? How would you write this in the story?

28

Unnecessary Precision

"The Difference That Doesn't Matter"

George: How old is this fossil?

Florence: One hundred million and five years.

George: How do you know that?

Florence: The sign says 100 million, but I've been working here for five years, and it was here when I got here.

DESCRIPTION OF THE ISSUE

When people use Unnecessary Precision, they are stating things with a level of precision that isn't actually possible to know. Often, overspecified numbers are used to suggest that speakers are more confident than they actually are or to be deceptive. For example, it's common for stores to price things at a dollar amount and 99 cents, and gas stations will even use tenths of a cent. This precision isn't needed and can encourage buyers to think that the item costs less than it actually does. It also makes pretty good jokes.

Humorist Dave Barry wrote a column on how to argue and gives the following example under the heading "Making things up":

> Suppose, in the Peruvian economy argument, you are trying to prove that Peruvians are underpaid, a position you base solely on the fact that you are underpaid, and you'll be damned if you're going to let a bunch of Peruvians be better off. Don't say "I think Peruvians are underpaid." Say instead: "The average Peruvian's salary in 1981 dollars adjusted for the revised tax base is $1,452.81 per annum, which is $836.07 below the mean gross poverty level." (Barry, n.d.)

Barry's joke depends on recognizing that framing a salary down to the penny makes a baseless argument seem like it is based on something. After all, where did those official-sounding numbers come from? Someone must know what they're talking about, right? Not exactly.

EXAMPLE

Sometimes, precision is implied where it is not really possible. A real-life example is found in calorie counts. Food packages and menus alike will list calorie counts to help consumers make good choices about the foods that they eat. Although this seems like a good idea in spirit, in practice, it can cause problems. There's a place called Biscuitville® where I sometimes like to eat breakfast on the weekends that serves breakfast sandwiches—some combination of meat, egg and cheese on their very tasty biscuits. The restaurant has calorie counts on the menu. Let's say I'm trying to be healthy, so I pick a bacon, egg and cheese biscuit at 440 calories instead of a sausage and egg biscuit at 480. It seems like a good choice, but those scratch-made biscuits I can watch the worker make by hand in the store do vary in size and in the amount of melted butter that gets brushed on the top. The eggs vary, too. In fact, in determining whether an egg is jumbo or peewee (a real egg classification!) or anything in between is done by weighing groups of eggs, not individual ones, so the individual ones could definitely vary a bit (USDA, 2000). Pretty soon, that 40-calorie difference could go away in differing sizes of the ingredients. It's the same with the calories per serving on a box. If I make a cake, I'm probably not going to get out the ruler and the protractor to make sure my slice is exactly one-eighth. The precise numbers in calorie counts aren't always meaningful and can cause people to make bad decisions.

COUNTERING THE UNNECESSARY PRECISION

If a source is using precise numbers, some critical thinking is in order, both for the truth and for the usefulness to the readers. In the example of the calorie counts, the counts were determined by a testing process that involved a sample sandwich at some point in the past. It's not possible to know how the sandwich in front of me compares to that one, if for no other reason than that the sandwich they measured was destroyed in the process of analyzing it. If I were writing a recipe to publish, I probably would want to keep my calorie counts general to be more accurate—between 400 and 500 calories might work. This could be more useful to the audience than a precise number I got by adding up the counts of the ingredients and dividing by the number of servings. If a source uses figures with Unnecessary Precision, don't quote their figures, rather, paraphrase them. For example, if the mayor says, "We're working for our hardworking citizens by lowering sales tax to 4.99 percent," you could paraphrase it as, "The mayor said the city sales tax will lower to about 5 percent." Take the time to consider the last few digits of precision: Are they accurate? Are they necessary? Are they potentially confusing or misleading? If so, reduce the precision in favor of accuracy and clarity.

YOUR TURN

1. Adnan Mevic's birth was heralded worldwide, and when he arrived, he got quite a welcome into the world. United Nations (UN) Secretary General Kofi Annan was at the hospital in Sarajevo, Yugoslavia, to pose for pictures marking the momentous time that the 6 billionth human took his first breaths. His birth was part of a "The Day of 6 Billion" that the UN encouraged nations to participate in, with books, media campaigns and websites released on his birthday, October 12 ("Secretary General to Welcome . . . ," 1999). A picture of Annan at the University Clinical Centre shows Annan cradling the baby, surround by blue and red flowers, and a banner over their heads reads, in English, "In this city I was born as the 6,000,000,000th person on our planet." If you were to share that picture, what would your caption be?

2. The European Union was discussing ways to make cars safer, but in the meantime, automakers were declining to take the initiative on their own (Tickell, 2005). In particular, cars were a lot better at keeping passengers safe but were not doing as well in terms of protecting pedestrians when they were in some kinds of collisions. Making the changes would be expensive for automakers but could save lives. Were the changes fully implemented, experts estimated that they would save 854 lives of walkers and cyclists and 36,917 injuries. But the automakers proposed a different standard that would mean 411 lives saved and 27,171 serious injuries. If you wrote a story about the negotiations, would you use these figures? What cautions might you feel about the precision of the numbers? Would that affect how you might write them in a story?

29

Naïve Probability and the Audience It Confuses

"This Slot Machine Is Hot"

Asha: I'm definitely not booking a flight with Gold Airlines.

Kwame: Why not?

Asha: They are the only airline that hasn't had a crash, so you know it must be their turn. My flight has to be next to crash.

DESCRIPTION OF THE ISSUE

If you go to a Las Vegas casino, you'll see that although table games like craps and roulette show up in movies a lot, a good bit of the floor is taken up with slot machines. These machines require different amounts of investment to spin the wheel and to gamble on getting a big payout. Sometimes people will watch the behavior of others on the floor, looking for a machine that has been in use for a long time. They hope that because the machine has taken in a lot of money, it's time for a big payout. Unfortunately, that's not how it works. Each time the wheels spin, the probability is the same, from the first spin of the day to the last. People are bad at understanding the likelihood of things occurring.

One of the biggest opportunities for exploiting Naïve Probability is people's understanding of risk. Here's an example: People worry about having to fight off a violent home invader, and some people spend hundreds of dollars on firearms they hope will keep them safe. According to recent crime statistics, only about 1 percent of homes are victims of burglaries at all, and homeowners are often not even at home to fight off the invader. When advertisements and editorials encourage listeners to buy firearms, they may take advantage of the audience's inability to judge the possibility of that risk.

It's not just the audience. Often, journalists also have a weak understanding of probability, which means that sometimes they overestimate risks when they report them. This gets compounded by the nature of news itself, which sometimes calls for highlighting the most spectacular of possibilities, even if it is not the likely one. The rare disease or improbable crime grabs the headlines, and to the audience, it appears to more likely just because of its prominence in the news.

Naïve Probability then is an issue in correctly conveying how likely a thing is to happen. The subject can be positive or negative. The problem can be ignorance or deception. But the real issue becomes the lack of understanding.

EXAMPLE

Divorce rates are pretty high, with between 40 and 50 percent of marriages breaking up, according to the National Marriage Project at the University of Virginia (National Marriage Project, n.d.). It would be easy to think, then, that of all of the couples who tied the knot this year 40 to 50 percent of them will break up. However, a marriage's likelihood of surviving depends on other factors about the bride and groom. Some factors that reduce the risk of divorce include having a higher income, not having a baby or being pregnant at the time of the marriage, being older than age 25 and having a college education. Another factor might be whether it is a first marriage for the bride and groom or a subsequent one, because second and third marriages are more likely to break up. This misinterpretation persists, though. Even recent news and feature stories, like McDowell (2017), still state a divorce rate of 50 percent like it applies to everyone. This can be confusing to audiences.

COUNTERING NAÏVE PROBABILITY

These kinds of mistakes can be really tough to combat. When you hear statements that give a range of possibilities and an average, it's important that you report the range and not just the average. You need to ask questions whenever there are probability explanations. To fail to do so is to risk confusing your audience. Brainard (2009) gives an example of a climate change story where the writer said the global temperature was expected to rise by at least 9 degrees. The figure was a median (a type of average) with a range that said it was 90 percent sure to be between 6.3 and 13.3 degrees. A reasonable way to write this is to say, "Scientists expect the climate to warm, giving 90 percent odds of an increase between 6.3 and 13.3 degrees by 2100." It might be tempting to report that it could rise as much at 13 degrees—more exciting and more clicks—but it's not responsible to do that. When reporting these kinds of stories, it is useful to ask for an explanation and make sure you get the source to give it in terms average readers can understand. Asking questions like "would you encourage a family member to . . . (have this surgery, do this activity, etc.)," can be a good way of getting an expert to put a risk in context. David Spiegelhalter, whose job is coming up with ways to help the public understand risk (Rathi, 2016), offers some tips. He suggests that putting things in whole numbers, like how many instances out of 100, can help make things clearer, as can using well-done charts (see chapter 30). Fuller (1996) suggests minimizing detail where possible can also help keep things clear for readers.

YOUR TURN

1. Statistician Darrell Huff (1954) gives an example from the Spanish-American War. During the war, the death rate for service members in the Navy was 9 in 1,000. For citizens living in New York at the same time, the death rate was 16 in 1,000. Huff states that military recruiters tried to use those figures to argue that people should join the Navy because it was safer than staying home. If you were writing a story about the recruiting drive, what questions would you ask? How would you contextualize the data in the story?

2. Several television game shows have used the principle of Naïve Probability to pull players through an emotional journey that makes for good television. *Deal or No Deal* was a popular television game show in which contestants faced a group of models holding numbered briefcases that contained signs with dollar amounts ranging from 1 cent to $1 million. The contestants took home whatever the last briefcase said. The catch was that every so often, a "banker" would offer to buy out the round, giving a suggestion of an amount of cash they would offer to entice the contestant to stop picking briefcases. The principle was the same as Vegas casinos where the house always wins. The banker's offer wasn't as good as the best the player could do if they happened to pick the best suitcase that was left, but the odds were against the player. If sharing how the game worked, how could you communicate the type of decision that the players faced?

30

Deception With Charts

"A Picture Is Worth 1,000 Lies"

Staffer Sara: The senator wants me to make a giant chart for her to present on the floor for the budget hearing showing that unemployment is way down.

Staffer Sandeep: How are you going to do that? It's actually way *up* since she took office.

Staffer Sara: Well, if I start during the 2009 recession, we look pretty good.

DESCRIPTION OF THE ISSUE

Sometimes pictures are a great help in understanding what is happening when dealing with information from numbers. Charts and graphs, in particular, can be an excellent way to see relationships that come from data. In 1992, Texas millionaire H. Ross Perot ran as an independent candidate for president. Lacking a history and platform as a politician, Perot spent hundreds of thousands of dollars to buy 30-minute blocks of air on TV during prime time to talk to the voters directly. He ran primarily on a balanced budget, and in just one of those sessions, he showed about two dozen charts illustrating assorted facts about the US economy as a part of his argument that a balanced budget was the most important campaign issue.

Politicians and businesspeople don't always use charts accurately. It's easy to create charts that look official but that don't tell the whole story. It's also easy to just make poor decisions in the choice of charts or graphs. For example, it's common to present budget figures as pie charts and even to create multiple pie charts to compare to show change. This is a bad way to visualize information because people have real difficulty appreciating how the size of the pie slices reflects the value of the underlying data. Poor graphs can make numbers confusing, and graphs can make numbers seem more official than the data quality supports. Always consider graphs and charts with suspicion.

EXAMPLES

Consider chart 1, which compares owner satisfaction for different brands of cars. The heading suggests that the owners of Studebakers are the most satisfied, according to J.D. Power rankings. You can see from the chart that Studebakers, on the left, are substantially better than many others in the top 10. But is it really? Notice the vertical y-axis on the chart. The range of scores is only from 31 to 39. It is misleading to say that Studebaker is much better because 1 or 2 points out of 40 may not be much better at all.

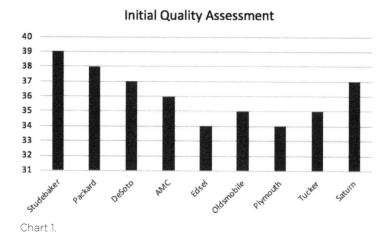

Chart 1.

Sometimes it is the look of the chart itself that can confuse reporters and audiences alike. Consider chart 2, which is a made-up visualization of data that looks like a common type: a pictograph in which the bars or columns are made of graphic representations instead of rectangles. In this case, it's intended that O'Brien (the larger boxer) has more wins, based on his height relative to Smith. Notice, though, that as a figure is taller on the vertical y-axis, it is also bigger—the volume changes drastically as well. Which element should the reader pay attention to? Height or volume? That's the problem with these kinds of charts.

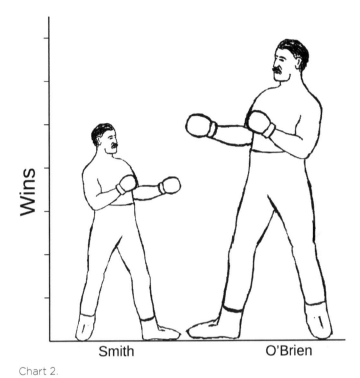

Chart 2.

There are entire books written on misleading data visualizations. Alberto Cairo's 2016 book and Gerald Jones's work from 2015 are good places to start to learn more.

DEALING WITH MISLEADING CHARTS

It's important to pay attention to charts because they can affect both your text and your visuals. Charts are generally representations of underlying numbers, and the best approach is to ask for or find the underlying data so you can see for yourself if the data is being presented fairly. A question you should ask yourself: *Is the data being shown related to the thing the person is claiming?* A chart of increasing SAT scores is great, but it doesn't tell you if graduates are earning acceptance to college. A chart of decreasing gas emissions doesn't tell you what is happening with global warming. Make sure the story, any captions on images and the headline focus on data related to the claim, even if the newsmaker presents information otherwise.

Let's return to the False Cause case of unemployment figures in chapter 26. Here is a potential chart of the falling unemployment rate continuing into 2018. Is the chart sufficient to understand the issue in context? Sometimes newsmakers will focus on a tiny part of a chart to make their record look better. Consider the following charts of US unemployment.

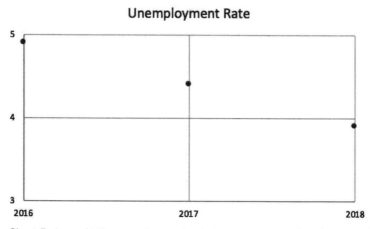

Chart 3. Annual US unemployment rate two years past the election of President Donald Trump

In chart 3, you see a clear reduction in the unemployment rate over three years. The journalist should ask some questions about this presentation. First, why is the vertical y-axis starting at three? This has the effect of making the drop appear more dramatic than it would if it started at zero.

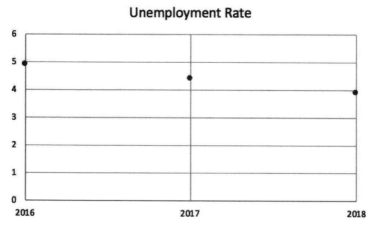

Chart 3a. Annual US unemployment rate two years past the election of President Donald Trump

The journalist would then ask why the speaker decided to start the chart at 3 percent. It might be because unemployment will not reach zero, but it also might be to make an argument that the election of President Donald Trump was good for unemployment. Does this chart support that argument? Maybe, but it doesn't make sense to start in 2016 because Trump became the president-elect in November of that year, meaning his election had little time to change business hiring practices or people's motivation to seek work or whatever the speaker argued. Speaking of context, let's look at another chart that the journalist could make for themselves after looking at the original data provided by visiting the Bureau of Labor Statistics website.

Unemployment Rate

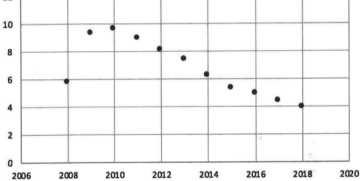

Chart 3b. Annual US unemployment rate traversing the 2009 financial crisis

This chart adds some important context. It is true that unemployment declined since Trump's election. But it's also true that this decline in unemployment is part of a larger pattern of increasing employment as the economy recovered from the 2009 financial crisis. When the journalist sees this pattern, it becomes clear that some more reporting needs to be done to present the facts truthfully. Simply repeating the claim in a story is doing the audience a disservice.

You should always be careful about including charts made by others. Whether you are a multimedia journalist or a mom with a Facebook account, be careful about sharing charts made by others, unless you have thoroughly vetted the data yourself. Even in the context of a story saying the claims are problematic, a misleading chart in the background may be all that your audience pays attention to, which means that you may be inadvertently spreading misinformation.

YOUR TURN

The National Weather Service creates maps of the likely path of hurricanes, but the paths are notoriously difficult to predict. The interaction of the rotation of the Earth and the temperatures and volumes of water at different locations mean that today's path might be well-known, but the destination five days from now, when it hits land, is much more speculative. The map tries to account for it with the cone of uncertainty, which is a visualization of where the center of the storm is likely to head.

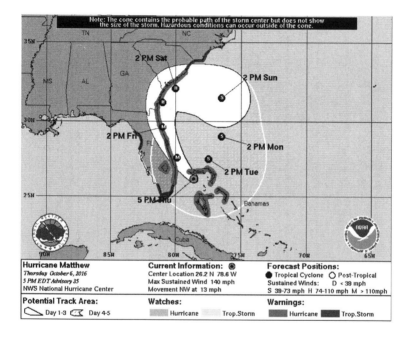

It's uncertainty for a reason: The center or eye of the storm could be anywhere within the visualized cone. Even that is not certain because it's a probability based on other recent storms. If you are sharing news about a storm, how would you contextualize this graphic for your audience? How would your answer change depending on whether your audience is inside or outside of the cone?

31

Misrepresenting Polls and Surveys

"Four out of Five Dentists Surveyed"

Daphne: I'm going to make so many changes when I'm club president!

Heathcliff: Aren't you getting ahead of yourself? We haven't even had the election yet!

Daphne: Well, we took a poll in my English class, and the polls say 51 percent are going to vote for me, so I'm going ahead and writing my acceptance speech.

DESCRIPTION OF THE ISSUE

Polls and surveys are a particular hazard in news for several reasons. First, when you are in a long-haul story like a political campaign, poll results can be a way to manufacture something that seems newsworthy because it has the news value of timeliness. Second, it's easy to misunderstand what the results of a poll even are. It's bad when the audience misunderstands a poll's value. It is even more unfortunate when the *journalist* misunderstands because the consequences of this misunderstanding can be severe, for example, voters choosing to stay home because they think their vote is irrelevant.

ISSUES WITH THE PEOPLE YOU ASK

When you want to know what a group of people think, you can try to interpret it from the things that they do, or you can ask them. Ideally, you do both, but the polling industry is based on asking people. When you have a group of any size, it quickly becomes too expensive and too difficult to ask everyone. Asking everyone is called a *census*, and there's a reason we only have one every 10 years in the United States; it's a massive, expensive undertaking. We still need to know what people think, so we get around this by taking a sample. The basic idea with polling is that a smaller group of people who are just like the population are asked questions to gather information for the larger group; this is called a *sample*. That way, it is assumed that each answer from the sample will be the same as the answers of some subset of the population. For example, if you want to know how people will vote, you might want to take a sample of likely voters. If you sample all Americans, you might get children or people who are legally prevented from voting, like convicted felons in some states. Sampling is a complicated topic, but you should generally know a few things:

- Most of the time, good sampling is random, which means that each person in the population has the same chance of being chosen for the survey.
- Samples will never represent the population as well as a census can, *but* well-chosen samples of an appropriate size can get close to representing the population accurately.

So the first thing to ask is *who* was asked and *how* were they chosen. Next, it's important to know *how* the questions were asked. Think about yourself for a moment. If a stranger wanted to reach you, what would be the best way? Do you even have a landline? Do you answer phone calls on your cell phone from numbers that you don't know? Do you read junk mail before you throw it away? If someone is standing on the street corner with a clipboard, do you approach them or cross the street? And are your answers typical of others of your age, occupation, race, income, education level or sex? There are different ways to ask people survey questions, and how you ask can affect who chooses to answer. If whole groups of people who have the attribute that you are studying are unlikely to answer, this makes the whole survey suspect. For example, it was controversial when the Trump administration proposed adding a question to the 2020 Census asking people about their citizenship (Mulvihill, 2019). The fear from critics was that people who are in the country illegally would fail to answer the Census questionnaires. This biases the responses and also risks undercounting the actual population in ways that matter. People who are in the country illegally may still drive on roads, visit the emergency department of local hospitals or send children to public schools. Federal grants help pay for some of these costs, and the allocation of those grants depends in part on population size.

Here's another example. If researchers are polling likely voters and decide to administer the poll on Snapchat, would this be a problem? If they are hoping to get a sample of all likely voters, then yes, it would be because older people are both likely to vote and less likely to use Snapchat. Just by choosing that technology, they are risking biasing the responses. If respondents select themselves for the survey, for example by choosing to answer poll questions on social media, the results could be the source for an amusing or cautionary feature but should not be reported as news.

There are different ways of asking people questions, and they come with different risks. Researchers can interview people or have them answer questionnaires face-to-face. Unless the population is contained—students in a single school, for instance—this is usually too expensive and time consuming. Imagine how hard it would be for researchers to ask questions in person for a sample of 1,000 people taken in the entire United States; it would require a month on airplanes. Telephone interviews are popular for pollsters. This is more complicated than it seems because numbers for businesses need to be left out, but pollsters have methods for that, and they know that phone polling is substantially more cost- and time-efficient. The issue is getting the people selected for the sample to actually answer the phone. A survey that only calls landlines, and there are some, becomes more suspect as the years pass simply because more and more citizens do not have home phones, preferring to go cellular only. Younger and lower-income people are both less likely to have landlines and risk being undercounted if cell phones are not included. Even if they are included in the survey, the prevalence of telemarketing and scams has made it increasingly likely that people won't answer phone calls from unknown numbers, and this can introduce bias as well. Online surveys are possible as well, through web browsers, apps and text messaging. This is also becoming complicated because people are unlikely to open "junk" e-mail and may have software set up to block it.

ISSUES WITH HOW YOU ASK

There can also be issues with the questions themselves. A questionable practice called "push polling" involves appearing to seek voter opinion but actually wording or ordering questions to affect voter opinion. A pollster could call and ask, "What's your opinion of Candidate Snodgrass's likely cheating on his taxes?" Even if Snodgrass did not cheat on his taxes, the idea is to plant a seed of distrust of Snodgrass that could later benefit his opponent, who sponsored the "poll." Around the time of the 2016 presidential elections, one campaign distributed a mainstream media bias survey through the US mail asking questions like how unfairly the media covered "our movement." Answering this question in any way is acknowledging that you feel like a member of this movement. For this reason, it's better to not report the results of internal polling or survey data, even if it is temptingly leaked to you. If you do report it, insist on seeing the original questions so you can provide context for the reader.

Bad questions aren't always a result of trickery on the part of the asker. Sometimes they are a problem because they are hard to answer. There's an entire field of research on how to ask good and bad questions, but there are a few things you can look for. First are double-barreled questions. If someone asks "Do you think the country should invest in infrastructure and security?," what does a "no" mean? For some respondents, it might mean they disagree with both. For others, it might mean they disagree with one but not the other. Because of this, it's hard to interpret what the respondent's answer means. Another issue is leading questions. If you ask "How much trouble was the city economy in before the new mayor took office?," you are asking the respondent to presume it was in at least some trouble. If you ask "Would you agree that Gupta has more relevant experience than Qing?," you are also leading because you imply that the experience opinion exists to be agreed with. A third issue is using absolute words like *always* and *never*. If you ask "Does Qing always make the best decisions for farmers?," it's hard for any respondent to answer "yes," if for no other reason because they may not be sure they know every decision Qing has ever made about farmers. It's a best practice to ask to see survey questions before you report results.

SHARING THE RESULTS OF POLLS

Everything so far has been about problems with polls caused by people—drawing bad samples or asking bad questions in bad ways. There's another type of error in the results that just comes from choosing to use a sample. Because of this error, the seemingly specific results in a poll based on a sample are never actually a certainty. They fall within a probability, and that can be important. There are two things to worry about: margin of error, which is commonly reported and confidence interval, which isn't. Let's say you get poll results that look like the following: Washington 49, Kardashian 51 (+/–3)

Can you report that Washington is ahead? Not at all. You do not know. The number next to each candidate is the midpoint of a range of possibilities, which is defined by the +/- number. Washington could get 48 percent, with Kardashian coming in at 52 percent. Or the exact opposite could happen, and Washington could be the winner, but there is no good way to know for sure. That +/– number is the margin of error—a range of possible results. So how do you know who will win?

You don't. You can't tell exactly which outcome is going to happen, but you have a pretty good feeling that that right answer is in that range. Pretty good feeling doesn't sound scientific at all. Really, the pretty good feeling is set up in advance when the pollster selects the size of the sample relative to the population. Basically, they are setting up a tolerance for how much they can risk being wrong, which they call the *confidence interval*. This is typically set at 95 percent. You can think about this as the number of times out of 100 that the answer for the population is within the range of results you found for the sample. In the preceding example, if we did polls with 100 different samples, we'd expect that 95 times, the opinions of the population were in the ranges given. How about the other 5 times? We just don't know. Pollsters and researchers don't always tell you the confidence interval, but if they don't, you should ask. If it's lower than 95 percent, don't report the results.

Finally, be really cautious about quoting from speeches and documents that refer to polls. Sometimes people refer to them and don't understand what they are referring to. Always get the original poll so you can check for yourself.

YOUR TURN

1. The results of the 2016 election surprised many people who followed polls leading up to Election Day, many of which showed Hillary Clinton having a persistent lead over Donald Trump. Here is a list of poll results, in percentage points, from the day before the election:

ABC News/*Washington Post*	Clinton by 5
Marist College	Clinton by 1
Fox News	Clinton by 2
NBC News/*Wall St. Journal*	Clinton by 4
Ipsos	Clinton by 4
IBD/TIPP	Trump by 1
CBS News/*New York Times*	Clinton by 3

These results, curated by numbers journalist Nate Silver on his fivethirtyeight.com site (2016), are for the polls that Silver rates as an A or A– in quality using a formula that considered how the polls are conducted and how accurate the poll has been in the past. Can you explain why these results can be reasonable in the face of Trump's election as president?

Appendix 1

Possible Answers to Section 1 Exercises

THERE ARE MANY WAYS TO WRITE A STORY, so your ideas may well be good ones. The model answers provided suggest ways that you might think about the statements and issues as well as ways you could handle the reasoning problems when sharing what the newsmaker said.

CHAPTER 1: THE PERSONAL ATTACK

1. Obama is saying that his opponents, the Republicans, were unqualified to make judgments about nuclear science because they are politicians and not nuclear scientists. Really, he is saying more. He is also accusing them of basing their views and actions on what their party has agreed to do instead of each fairly considering the question. He is also saying they are thinking more about the image they could garner on TV than the things that might result from their decisions. These are attacks on the opponents and their motivations rather than a refutation of the ideas that the opponents had, so it is a Personal Attack. To contextualize this story, you could do some background investigation. It would be appropriate to look at the time line of Republican criticism: Was it in fact so early that critics could not have read and considered the proposal? You could include the dates of critical remarks and press releases so readers could judge for themselves. It's also worth finding out who those "lobbyists and pundits" actually are. Do they have qualifications to speak about nuclear technologies and strategies? They might, in which case, it would be useful for the opponents to listen to them. In explaining this speech to your audience or deciding to share it on social media, you could explain what the president meant and share who the people were so your audience could decide.

2. Schwarzenegger is using a cultural reference here that most people at the time would have been familiar with—a *Saturday Night Live* skit that had characters that mimicked Schwarzenegger's accent and acted like weight lifters who insulted people who didn't work out by saying a person might be a "girlie man." This kind of cultural reference makes a story interesting, and a story about the governor using that language could get a lot of clicks because it is unusual and attention-getting. However, the journalist has done the readers a disservice if they leave it there. Calling legislators "girlie men" is a Personal Attack, but it is hiding a bigger attack that needs to be examined because it is definitely in the public interest. Schwarzenegger is saying that legislators are basing their decisions on powerful people in society who provide campaign money or exert influence on large blocks of voters that will help keep those legislators in office. Is this true? Before you repeat Schwarzenegger's words, you need to find out. A reporter could ask exactly what special interests are being supported by which legislators. Reporters or citizens could be looking up the priorities of unions, trial lawyers, and so on and asking the legislators or their staffs their views on those issues. Finally, if you interview the legislators about the governor's remarks, don't settle for comments about how government figures should have respectful discussions. Do the legislators believe they are acting for groups other than the citizens? Do they believe that what the unions want is in the interest of all citizens in their districts? Why?

CHAPTER 2: POISONING THE WELL

1. Kennedy is trying to make the listener assume that because Nixon was nominated by a particular political party, he would necessarily adopt and advocate for all of the Republican Party policies. This might be a reasonable assumption—after all, parties use the same political convention where they nominate their candidates to develop their platforms, which are a set of values and priorities that members of the party agree they will work toward. In this case, though, Kennedy is Poisoning the Well by asking the audience to believe that anything Nixon says is just the same Republican point of view. This is an untested assumption and, probably, an unfair one as well. In a country that was less than 200 years old, 25 years is a substantial length of time, and it is likely that party priorities shifted some during that time. Note that Kennedy tries to cover for this by stating that it is "most" of the 25 years. There are still two assumptions here that need to be addressed in context for a story or before sharing Kennedy's statement. First, does Nixon, in fact,

intend to do whatever the party agrees on while in office? Has he made statements about that? Could you get a question answered or look at past behavior to see? Second, are those actions over the 25 years, in fact, the ones Republicans would support today? Voting records for Republican legislators or even previous news articles could help answer this question.

2. It is true that Cohen was a convicted felon and one of the charges to which he pled guilty was lying to Congress about a deal he was working on for the president to build an office tower in Moscow. However, reminding the committee and the watching audience for this live televised hearing of his convictions and going on to state that Cohen was invited by a friend of Trump's 2016 political opponent is an example of Poisoning the Well. Jordan is implying that because Cohen has lied in the past, he will not tell the truth now. Cohen's statements, Jordan implies, should be evaluated based on Cohen's character rather than their content. Jordan is Poisoning the Well, which may cause any fact Cohen shares to be rejected out of hand. As a journalist covering this hearing, you can quote Cohen's statements, even if he lies, because of privilege. However, it is your job to do your best to verify things that he says and to provide context about the statements, how seriously they were taken and what it might lead to for Congress. More than that, it is useful to identify Jordan's statements as attempting to discredit Cohen as a witness and to point out that members of the committee did or did not say they will investigate Cohen's claims further.

CHAPTER 3: THE STRAW MAN

1. The thing that is working is Obama's health care plan. Those who said no one would sign up are the Republican opponents to the plan. In fact, the plan was not widely beloved in Congress when it passed; it was a challenge even to get all Democrats to support it. In reporting this story, facts and nuance are both important. The journalist needs to ask the speaker who "they" are when it comes to who said no one would sign up. Once that is identified, it's useful to see if lack of citizen interest in enrolling was a real part of Republicans determining whether they would support the bill. If that isn't a part of speeches or content of floor debates, the reporter needs to make that clear in the story.

2. Clinton is stating an opinion of an unnamed opponent. It's your job to give that opponent a name, preferably by asking a follow-up question either to the source or a spokesperson. If the source can't provide one, don't print the quote.

CHAPTER 4: THE APPEAL TO HYPOCRISY

1. In this case, Kavanaugh is trying to deflect questions about his drinking onto Klobuchar to make it seem like drinking to the point of blackout is normal. Remember that the line of questions was intended to see if Kavanaugh might be capable of recalling his actions in high school at the party about which Blasey Ford made the accusation. You will notice, reading the transcript of the exchange, that Kavanaugh does not ever answer the question of whether he has ever been blackout drunk. His attempt to ask Klobuchar if she had similar issues while drinking is trying to show that his past behavior was not bad—maybe everyone does it. His indirect answer to Klobuchar's question seems newsworthy. In this case, because an ability to remain objective and to understand arguments is relevant to service as a Supreme Court Justice, the entire exchange also seems to be relevant. Although probably not worth the space to print the whole exchange, a summary could be useful to readers. For example, "Senators tried to determine if Kavanaugh's behavior with alcohol while in high school could explain the different statements by Kavanaugh and Blasey Ford. Senator Amy Klobuchar asked Kavanaugh if he had ever been drunk enough to have memories lapse. After asking the senator if she had ever done that, Kavanaugh never answered her question."

2. Fleischer's tweet is certainly inflammatory, but it may not be newsworthy in and of itself, especially if the story is about Barr's show cancellation. If it were a second-day story covering consequences for rude speech, the Tweet might be relevant, if put into context. For example,

> Critics suggest that different parties are treated differently when it comes to consequences for speech. Former George W. Bush press secretary Ari Fleischer tweeted "Compare ABC's reaction to Roseanne Barr's tweet w TBS's non-reaction to Samantha Bee and you'll see a double-standard in action. There's no uprising against Bee. Why? Because she is liberal. Because the MSM protects Obama and his aides, but not Trump. The hypocrisy is sickening."

CHAPTER 5: THE RED HERRING

1. Clinton definitely did not answer the question. To report it, you can say something like, "When Blitzer asked the candidates if they would consider a president/VP ticket with the other, Clinton did not answer, instead reminding viewers of a town hall her campaign scheduled for next week."

2. Romney did not answer the question about pay equity. His answer is still relevant, however, because it provides important insight into his views on women in the workplace and was, in fact, widely reported, largely because of some phrasing that some audiences found objectionable. Reporting his answer would need both some context and summary. For example,

> Romney didn't directly answer a question about pay equity for women. He spoke at some length about his experience as governor, where, he said, he found that there were not any women applying for jobs in the Cabinet so he asked women's groups to help find qualified candidates. "They brought us whole binders full of women," Romney said. He also talked about the need to have a strong economy that would provide more jobs for all, including women, and that would encourage employers to provide flexible hours.

CHAPTER 6: THE BLACK AND WHITE

1. Bush's words are definitely quotable and were said to make a strong impact. What Bush said does reflect Black and White logic, but that doesn't mean a story on this speech is a good place to point that out. The either–or thinking implies that the issue of terrorism is a simple one, ignoring the fact that the definition of terrorism is not a universally agreed-upon one. Further, all conflicts have multiple sides. What your team sees as a win, the other team will see as a loss. Basically, there are other sides to this story. However, in a story about the speech, it would be hard to include these kinds of nuanced issues. It would be good to plan for follow-up stories that could go into more depth about the conflicts that led to the moment.

Bush's words also suggest that people, groups or nations need to get involved in other people's battles. In this particular case, Bush stated that other nations needed to actively fight with the United States against terrorism. If this means joining military actions, this is a quite large request that could involve leaders taxing their own public and perhaps costing lives of their citizens. Bush is making a vague threat here, stating that nations that don't join the fight will have consequences. This is worth a follow-up question about what exactly is meant by being "held accountable" and by "inactivity," the answers to which should run in the first story about the speech. The reader will also benefit from context about treaties and other historical mutual defense arrangements that might apply here, but this context could be better served in an in-depth, second-day story.

2. Obama is offering a Black and White choice: Either take this deal now or face a war soon. There is no evidence from history that war is inevitable, and the evidence that Iran was enriching uranium with the intent of declaring war was also lacking. Some experts even suggested that a vague threat of maybe working toward nuclear weapons gives a country more bargaining power than a certainty that they are. As a reporter, it's appropriate to ask for additional information about why Obama was making that claim. If a quote from the president isn't available, interviewing experts or even looking up background research could help you to provide this context. A sentence stating, "Although Obama's remarks make it sound like war is the inevitable other option, experts disagree." After this, you could provide clarification or other expert opinion. It also might be worth a quote from people who opposed the agreement by giving their view on whether war is the inevitable alternative.

CHAPTER 7: THE SLIPPERY SLOPE

1. This one is tricky, and it's important to note that Sean Hannity has an opinion program that runs on the Fox News cable channel. He is not acting as a journalist. A journalist might try to include Hannity's remarks as a part of a story on reaction to a potential gun ban. With respect to his comment on about Britain and Australia, the implication that law-abiding citizens in Britain cannot own firearms for protection isn't accurate, and the journalist needs to make that clear. Considering Australia, Hannity's implication is correct. Private citizens can own guns but must demonstrate a reason, and protection isn't considered a fair reason (Cohen, 2012, para 11).

When it comes to the proposed US gun regulations following the Las Vegas shooting, Pelosi herself said something vague about what some members want to do with those regulations. For Hannity to conclude that, "They want to ban all guns" is the end of a Slippery Slope that is not supported by the public statements on guns from many members of Congress that can be easily located in election speeches. At the very least, stories should note this to contextualize Hannity's remarks. Ideally, it would be of interest to interview someone from Pelosi's staff to get an idea of specifics on the "many more things."

2. The first event Hickson notes is the modern Puritan mania, including prohibition and other behavior controls. The end is becoming a nation of degenerates, a result of the weakening of males by trying to impinge on their behavior. Process in the steps isn't clear because he focuses on effects. It's relevant to state that Hickson doesn't state exactly

how prohibition leads to a falling birth rate. When he states that the birth rate is already falling, you'd want to check and see if that is true, and if so, if there are other explanations. For example, times of economic crisis tend to result in lower birth rates because people delay having children until they are sure they can afford their care.

CHAPTER 8: THE FALLACY OF FALLACIES

Answers will vary.

CHAPTER 9: THE FAULTY ANALOGY

1. In this situation, you are looking at more than a reasoning issue. Clinton's statement is arguably an example of a Faulty Analogy: She's implying that her hard work will lead to winning, but the comparison is a fictional character that worked hard yet lost. In this case, though, Clinton's use of a bad analogy, although unfortunate, doesn't really detract from the main point that she said she was a fighter. There might be a point to make about the depth of her interest in Philadelphia compared to simple pandering in choosing a movie about a working-class boxer in Philadelphia when speaking to union members in the city. This would be a better point for a larger story on how this candidate, or all candidates, try to appeal to local crowds, which is a pretty common news feature during the primaries.

More than a reasoning issue, using an unnecessary quote to point out a logical error becomes an ethical issue. If the quote isn't essential to the speaker's argument, you should consider the portion of the Society of Professional Journalists' Code of Ethics relating to minimizing harm. As the code states, "Balance the public's need for information against potential harm or discomfort. Pursuit of the news is not a license to arrogance or undue intrusiveness." Although it could be argued that being a candidate for president creates a newsworthiness or a public need for information for statements and actions, that newsworthiness is not absolute. Clinton's gaffe might be newsworthy in a story about pandering candidates, but in the context of a speech to a labor union, it is arguably not. You can safely choose to not report this logical problem at all.

2. Johnson is also speaking to a labor union, but in this case, his statement is germane to the facts of the issue. He was asked if the United States could reasonably focus on matters at home and on matters abroad. He made the analogy of his daughters, who require the care of

their parents. The needs of offspring are not at all comparable to the needs of a nation or region and the resources of the Johnsons are not at all comparable to the resources of the entire United States. He did not address Meany's concerns.

Johnson's comparison seems reasonable, but it is actually a Faulty Analogy because the two aren't comparable. In a follow-up question, you could ask something like, "You said that we have to meet foreign and domestic problems head-on. Can you provide some specific ideas for how that might work?" You could also ask, "What are your estimates of the amount of money needed for your anti-poverty plan? Where will that money come from?" If you don't get those questions answered in time for publication, you could paraphrase, saying something like, "Responding to Meany's question, Johnson said the nation had to meet both domestic and foreign obligations, but didn't provide specifics on how US resources might rise to meet both needs."

CHAPTER 10: THE IRRELEVANT CONCLUSION

1. While 42 years is, indeed, a long time to be married and may, in fact, be an indication of "steadiness and constancy," it is not *political* steadiness, which was the nature of the question. Although Romney's information was true, it was not relevant. It would be possible to ask if Romney was making a joke, which is possible. If not, it's reasonable to ask, "Why would faithfulness in marriage be the same as making consistent decisions while in office?" If you don't have the opportunity to get that clarification, you could write something with context like, "Harwood asked Romney to comment on the consistency of his opinions over time, noting that the candidate had, had several notable changes of mind. Romney responded by noting the length of his marriage, suggesting it showed he was a man of 'steadiness and constancy.'"

2. The tweet suggests an Irrelevant Conclusion. Caslen may have some higher education, military success and, possibly, also a distinguished record at West Point. West Point is not a major research institution like the University of South Carolina, which creates a question if Caslen's experience is truly relevant. Further, military experience is a valued type of leadership, but university faculty and staff don't necessarily respond to leadership in the same way that military staff and civilian employees would. It might be reasonable to use this tweet as part of a story about the controversy about the hiring, but the story would need to make the differences in institutions and leadership between the institutions clear.

CHAPTER 11: THE HASTY GENERALIZATION

1. You could use Gore's quote, but it would be important for you to put it in context. The fact that people with criminal records in Texas were able to get guns is concerning, but Texas is only 1 of 50 states. This gets complicated because there may not be a simple comparison group because the study may have only been done in Texas (the home of George W. Bush). This doesn't negate the logic issue. If time permits, the journalist should investigate to see if a broader study had been done to contextualize Gore's words. If time was short, it is worth it to note the source of Gore's statistic and the limitations of its size. "Gore said 'too many criminals are getting guns. There was a recent investigation of the number in Texas who got—who were given concealed weapons permits in spite of the fact that they had records,' citing a *Los Angeles Times* article. Texas may not be representative of the situation around the country," could be a good way to handle it in a night-of story about the debate.

2. Reagan repeated this story in multiple speeches because he wanted the audience to believe that there was a systematic problem of welfare abuse. He was using a shocking example to make the audience feel like if one person can get away with it, that can't be the only example. Once audiences believe that the situation may not be unique, they might become more sympathetic to his idea for welfare reform to prevent widespread abuse. It kind of worked, as well. Borrelli (2019) writes that the *Chicago Tribune* used the term in more than 80 stories, including those about Linda Taylor, the woman Reagan was talking about. Taylor was shorthand for Reagan, but a book (Levin, 2019) showed that her case was unique and complex. However, the existence of Taylor doesn't mean that there is, in fact, a larger problem, even if she were as the candidate described. Reagan does not provide enough evidence of a systematic problem because he is making a Hasty Generalization. Reagan should be asked how he knows that Taylor is an example of others and what evidence he has that the issue extends beyond this one case in Chicago. If you wanted to include the remarks in a story and could not do an interview or background research for context, you could say something like, "Reagan's description of a woman in Chicago was the only evidence the candidate offered that a national issue with welfare abuse means that reform is needed."

CHAPTER 12: THE DIVISION FALLACY

1. There are several reasoning issues in Trump's statement. He is trying to say that the views of US women justify an aggressive immigration

policy. The statement that women want security assumes that because one belongs to the group of women, one wants security. This could be a Division Fallacy, but, as stated, probably is not. However, there is an implication that having migrants in general or asylum seekers in particular is, in some way, reducing security. If you say being a woman means you hold this view or that you "don't want to have those people in our country," you are almost certainly assuming the attitude is held by all women. You'd want to know how the president arrived at that view about women. Is he referring to poll results? Anecdotal media accounts? If you are going to repeat his statement to your audience, it would be good to also explain why he holds those views about women.

2. Pan is stating that parents and others who oppose vaccines do so because they lack information about vaccines. Although some anti-vaccine views are driven by incorrect information about the risks of side effect—a belief in a debunked theory about a link with autism and the like—this is not the only reason people oppose vaccines. For example, as the question states, religious belief and worry about governmental overreach also play a role. It's not entirely certain that more information about vaccine safety will change the minds of everyone who opposes them. Assuming that someone belonging to the group of people who object to vaccines is misinformed is an example of the Division Fallacy. Knowing that there are other reasons why these people choose not to vaccinate could be the basis of a good interview with Pan, and you could ask him about what might be helpful in the face of religious objections and the like.

CHAPTER 13: THE COMPOSITION FALLACY

1. Bachmann is seeking support for tougher laws dealing with undocumented immigrants and, in particular, using the Franco example as a way of suggesting that undocumented immigrants are a crime risk and threat to safety. The *New York Times* reported an analysis (Flagg, 2019) that crime rates don't increase as the number of undocumented migrants increase, suggesting that Bachmann is making a Composition Fallacy by assuming that because one migrant's actions had tragic outcomes, allowing migrants means allowing tragedies, thus migration as a whole needs to be addressed. It would be appropriate to ask what evidence Bachmann had that tougher immigration policies would lead to less crime. Although dealing with the fallacy surrounding the trend, it's important to keep the particulars in mind as a part of sensitive reporting. The death of four children in a school bus accident is, indeed, tragic, and the person who hit the bus was, in fact, in the country illegally.

2. People will act in ways contrary to their own personal beliefs all the time, from the advertising copywriter who hates smoking but writes copy about cigarettes to the religiously conservative nurse who provides care for a pregnant teenager. Robinson has a point that law enforcement should not contribute to any kind of violence. But the presence of people with white supremacist beliefs in police forces does not mean that the police force as a whole can't enforce equal treatment under the law. That is a question that needs to be investigated by looking at the records of action of law enforcement agencies. The belief that an organization will necessarily take on the characteristics of some members is a Composition Fallacy. Follow-up questions you could ask would be asking for more evidence: "Are there records that show that police forces with white supremacist officers act differently in the field?" There's a second important issue, and it's also worth asking, "What effect does having white supremacist officers have on diverse groups in the community?"

CHAPTER 14: BEGGING THE QUESTION

1. Rubio says that his parents' jobs existed and this proves free enterprise is effective. To fully expand his argument, free enterprise works; therefore, his parents had jobs; and hence, free enterprise works. Really, the fact that his parents were employed could be a result of any number of factors, which is, in itself a problem with the reasoning. He is assuming that the presence of jobs indicates that free enterprise works, when in fact it might be equally plausible that they got jobs for another reason such as a family member employing them or being part of a government program. Saying his parents had jobs is not sufficient, and he doesn't provide other evidence. The Begging the Question is because Rubio is saying free enterprise works, therefore, free enterprise works. To use this section of the speech in a story, you would not want to repeat the inadequate justification, perhaps cutting the quote like this: "Rubio said that if he were elected 'We are going to have a president that embraces a free economy.'"

2. Kennedy's word is unfortunate here. Essentially, he is saying that unity is powerful because it is cooperative. Most people would find that cooperation has at least some element of unity to it. Then, this would say to be united is to be united, which is Begging the Question. This is an effort at rhetorical drama rather than an effort to be deceptive. In a story, you could use a quotation like this without causing much damage. You could also simply paraphrase by saying something like, "Kennedy said national unity would allow the country to succeed."

CHAPTER 15: THE APPEAL TO PURITY

1. Dunn is speaking against Republican critics of President Roosevelt, but his words "No true American" suggest that support for the president should be because of desire for in-group status rather than because of the president's actions. It assumes that the biggest responsibility of citizenship is cheerleading the status quo, thus is an Appeal to Purity. This is a case in which some follow-up questions are useful, including things like whether dissent is ever patriotic, whether one could ever rightly criticize the government and if those who criticize the government are not true Americans, what are they?

2. Fazio says "true Americans" have a "commitment to fairness, justice, and basic human rights." Even if this is true, his statement suggests that particular behaviors are needed to demonstrate that commitment, in particular allowing Haitians to stay in the United States. It would be helpful to ask for clarification on this issue. Migration and accommodating refugees are complicated issues that do cost a receiving country in resources. Additionally, a country has other options to encourage a repressive government to support its citizens like economic sanctions or foreign aid. A reporter could ask Fazio for additional details on why allocating those resources to maintain Haitians represents fairness and justice. He could also be asked why other definitions of fairness and justice might not be American and if there were other conceivable ways to demonstrate a commitment to human rights. If it is not possible to ask follow-up questions, it is important to make it clear that it was Fazio's argument that true American values meant allowing refugees to stay.

CHAPTER 16: EQUIVOCATION

1. The words *sexual relations* are the example of Equivocation. For most people, sexual relations implies, but doesn't specify, sexual intercourse. That's not what happened in the case of Clinton and Lewinsky. By using a suggestive term (no pun intended), Clinton was hoping to get away with a technical truth while ignoring the understood meaning. He was trying to be deceptive—a decision that was later found out. His making a similar denial in front of a grand jury eventually formed the first article of his impeachment by the House (the Senate failed to convict, and Clinton remained in office). This kind of Equivocation is hard to detect in an interview situation. If a reporter noticed the odd wording, Clinton could be asked what exactly was meant by the term.

2. Is torture, torture? Does calling it something else change what it is? Bush is trying to redefine torture by equivocating the meaning to

be things that are illegal. The argument is essentially that because the intentions of the action are to fight terrorism, that is, by definition, legal and, therefore, not torture. This also seems like an effort to deceive. A follow-up question should be, "Which definition of torture are you using when you say that?" Before sharing that quote, it is important to answer that question and to share that there was a US opinion on what torture was and to explain how that opinion was similar to and different from the United Nations' agreed-upon definition.

CHAPTER 17: THE SUNK COST

1. What is the goal for visiting the fancy buffet? The answer to this will help determine if a Sunk Cost Fallacy is involved. These luxurious buffets are known for having some foods that people don't eat regularly at home—prime steaks, crab legs, desserts like baked Alaska and more. If the goal is to enjoy fancy treats, eating two meals for the price of one might be a poor strategy because there's a bit of a diminishing return on how much you enjoy food as you fill up. Eating too much rich food because you paid a lot for it is thinking tainted by a Sunk Cost fallacy. However, if your goal is to get a good value on feeling very full, you might accomplish this by sneakily eating twice for one price, as the article suggests. "You will be full afterwards; that's the whole idea!"

2. As Bush notes in his speech, war has real costs, and the loss of human lives is a serious one. Particularly for an audience of veterans who have, perhaps, lost friends and colleagues in conflicts, it is definitely worth acknowledging this. However, if a war is going to drag on, unwinnable, then the lives lost don't seem like they would justify continuing to put people in danger. The loss of life is tragic, but it is already done and future action can't undo it. As stated, Bush's justification seems like an example of a Sunk Cost fallacy. If there is a reason to believe that future actions would result in victory, it might be useful to persist despite continued cost, but that argument isn't found here. It would be useful to ask for evidence of why the conflict will have a successful outcome. As a note to the reader, Bush gave this speech in 2005. At the time of writing of this book in 2020, the United States still had thousands of troops stationed in both Afghanistan and Korea.

Appendix 2

Possible Answers to Section 2 Exercises

CHAPTER 18: THE APPEAL TO PITY

1. Clinton is making a clear Appeal to Pity here, one that's common in the face of government shutdowns. In a shutdown, the members of Congress, who have the "power of the purse" to fund government operations, are unable to agree enough to pass a spending bill before the last funding runs out, and thus, the government literally runs out of spendable money. No money means an inability to pay workers, who are temporarily told to stay home unpaid. As Clinton points out, many civil servants are decent sorts who do their job with integrity but face more uncertainty because of the unique way the government pays for things. Isn't it a shame that these decent people get treated this way is the Appeal to Pity here.

Is this appeal likely to work in the face of congressional disagreement? It might make some difference, but the temporary perils of individual employees are issues that funders may see as less important than issues like debt control or providing particular programs important to voters (or campaign donors). In any case, Dean's individual story is an interesting and moving one, but not central to government funding issues broadly, which is what matters in getting a budget passed. His story could be a good one as a sidebar to a larger piece on budget negotiations, but in the context of a speech story about the State of the Union, it might be better to say that the president reminded Congress of the contributions of dedicated federal employees, using them to ask Congress to "Never, ever shut down the Federal government again."

2. This quote by Ryan is an Appeal to Pity and surprising because of the power and responsibility of the president. A reporter would have

many follow-up questions for the majority leader, including whether Ryan actually felt like the president's actions were wrong (a question he did not actually answer), and if the action was wrong, whether inexperience should excuse these kinds of actions and what the role of government experts should be in helping elected officials act in line with laws and policies. Even if the reporter doesn't get to ask those questions, Ryan's quote is worth including because it raises those kinds of issues. Information on the propriety of the action could come from other sources like government ethics officials, as could the role of nonelected staff who, presumably, are experienced.

CHAPTER 19: THE APPEAL TO FORCE

1. An Appeal to Force is arguing that going along with the speaker is necessary to avoid terrible consequences and the threats Bush is arguing are, indeed, terrible. Iraqi dictator Hussein already demonstrated his access to poisonous gases in an attack on the town of Halabja in his own country, in which at least 5,000 people died. The town has a monument to the event, which happened in 1988. Bush's evidence falls short of demonstrating that there is a real, imminent threat to the United States of either of these perils. Implying that there is, with the evidence being agreement by members of Congress and members of the United Nations Security Council, is an Appeal to Force that may be in bad faith. The president doesn't even indicate how many members of Congress and the council actually agree with him. If you share the quote about the specifics of the threat, it needs to be bracketed with context about how likely those threats actually are. At the time the speech was given, both in the United States and the world, the threat of nuclear weapons and other weapons of mass destruction was highly debated. This would need to be included along with the quote.

2. Kennedy is arguing that the United States should allocate more money on foreign affairs in support of Berlin. The nation was already investing in Asia in an effort to combat a threat of communism there. Kennedy's logic is that if the same amount of money in the budget was just moved to assist Berlin, that would help communists in Asia. The country needed forces in both places, or communism would become a problem in whichever place wasn't being helped. "We can't afford not to meet this challenge," is a vague threat, but still an Appeal to Force. It would be helpful to audiences to detail what specific threats there would be for the millions of people in West Berlin, the part not controlled by communists, and what specific threats there are in Asia.

CHAPTER 20: THE APPEAL TO IGNORANCE

1. Stam's argument is relying on the assumption that if something is consequential, legislators will have filed bills to make laws about it. Because he can't find this specific kind of evidence that people find it important, it must not actually be important, he says, which is an Appeal to Ignorance. Stam's assumption is flawed in a few ways. First, there are many things people care about but don't make laws about. Because no one has proposed a law that all people are required to own dogs, does that mean that members of the public don't value dogs as pets? A second flaw is that urgency of the issue is the only matter that would cause a legislator to introduce a bill. Other factors like how realistic it would be for the bill to get passed also play a role. In reporting on this panel, you could leave Stam's quote out entirely. At the event, some follow-up questions about why Stam felt no one introduced such a bill or what else lack of a bill could mean could help provide nuance to his views. Finally, if that quotation is shared, it needs to have context. It seems like Stam is stating the number of bills to make an impression by using a large number. Is it a large number in the context of the history of state lawmaking? What is the topic of most bills that are introduced? Are bills to repeal *any* law common?

2. Dukakis is trying to malign Bush's character by stating that he hasn't seen Bush advocate for Senate sessions to start with the Pledge of Allegiance. There are several assumptions contained in Dukakis's statement that form the basis of a bad faith argument. First, Dukakis is affirming "to the best of my knowledge," which is a nebulous standard. It would be useful for the reporter to find out if it actually had happened. Second, there is context missing. The Vice President is the presiding officer of the Senate, but does that mean he usually attends sessions? Was this the case for Bush? Would the Vice President as presiding officer be the one who would actually suggest this? The audience needs to know this context. Finally, Dukakis is presuming that the proof of patriotism needed is recommending the Pledge of Allegiance in government proceedings. This seems overly specific and intended more to hurt the Vice President than to make a valid point.

CHAPTER 21: THE APPEAL TO AUTHORITY

1. Schaivo's case was a tragic one for all involved. Frist might seem to have additional authority to speak on the medical facts of the case by virtue of his training as a physician. However, once doctors complete a general training in medical school, there is substantial training in areas

of specialty, after which the physician will generally work nearly exclusively in that specialty. Frist could be a highly competent transplant surgeon, but this training is not the same as advanced training in neurology. Consider the reverse: Would you want a trained neurologist performing your kidney transplant? Although Frist's views might matter more than that of a member trained as a lawyer, using them exclusively would be risking a bad judgment based on Appeal to Authority. His view might indicate that evaluation by a trained neurologist would be useful, but it isn't enough in itself. A story on the Senate deliberations should make this clear, along with stating the findings of the neurologists who had participated in Schaivo's care.

2. Schaefer is stating that the right to possess guns in Texas is given by God, and Milano is objecting to that statement and asking for an argument from Christian scripture to support the statement. Like many arguments that take place in character-limited social media, these arguments are not fully fleshed out. Cruz's reply tries to answer the scripture question and use governmental language. The Declaration of Independence does say:

> We hold these truths to be self-evident, that all men are created equal, that they are endowed by their Creator with certain unalienable Rights, that among these are Life, Liberty and the pursuit of Happiness.

Cruz's use of scripture does, perhaps suggest that under a scriptural standard, defense of property is OK with God. There's a long way from that to a God-given right to own weapons or modern firearms. Stories about Twitter spats sometimes happen because they get views that earn money for a publication, but they also can have little news value. If you did choose to share this controversy, you would need to make it clear that the arguments are limited because the Declaration of Independence is a position statement and not a governing document. As such, using it as an argument for law is a bad Appeal to Authority. You would also want to note that the scripture Cruz cites doesn't actually say anything about weapons.

CHAPTER 22: THE APPEAL TO TRADITION

1. Santorum is arguing that human history is the evidence that male-female parenting is best for children. This is a typical Appeal to Tradition argument: It has always been that way, so it should be that way in the future. It's not sufficient because there's a second problem with his argument as well: The question is not about who is raising children but

rather about legal marriage as defined by the Supreme Court. When Santorum claims there is a problem that hurts children because people now believe marriage is not about having children, that doesn't necessarily follow logically. If you accept his first premise that having children raised by mixed-sex parents is best, that doesn't mean that the thousands of years of human history he cites pertain to legal definitions of marriage. Because being married is not a prerequisite for having and raising children, his argument doesn't really apply. If you were doing a story about the candidate, it would probably be better to paraphrase rather than quote him on these matters, making it clear in the paraphrase that the matters are separate. For example, "In an interview, Santorum said he would favor overturning a Supreme Court ruling that legalized gay marriage. He also said he thinks children do better when raised by mixed-sex parents."

2. In this case, Reses is offering assertions without proof, but it doesn't actually fit in the category of Appeal to Tradition because the argument is lacking evidence. If writing a news piece about the move, you would want to ask for that evidence. How does the company know that communication, collaboration, speed and quality are better when employees are at the same location? In particular, you'd want to know if the decision was based on Yahoo! history, history in the industry or some other factor.

CHAPTER 23: THE APPEAL TO POPULARITY

1. Sanders is arguing that all the other "major" countries have guaranteed health care for all citizens. Because the rest of the industrialized world has done it, we should as well. This is an Appeal to Popularity because the evidence offered here is just that others are doing it. It's used a lot for policy matters like health, work hours and maternity leave. It's not a sufficient argument because whatever it means to be "major" does not mean all countries that qualify are alike in their need for or their ability to provide particular things to citizens. He is essentially providing evidence that it works in other countries by virtue of the fact that the countries have kept the practice. The United States is different from other countries in some ways that might matter such as population size, population density and more. If you were doing a story on this, you'd want some evidence that universal health care could work effectively here, asking questions about what things work in other countries that would or would not work here and why.

2. Nixon is stating that his obligation is to make the best decision, meaning the one that is liked by this "silent majority" he describes, which looks like a classic Argument to Popularity. There are a couple

of concerns here. First, it's not clear that good military decisions are the decisions endorsed by the most people at home because the great majority of those people aren't experts. Second, if the majority is silent, how do you know what they want? It is a big assumption that not protesting equals endorsement, and it's not supportable. It might be that some citizens of San Francisco had to work that day or were sick, yet still opposed the war. It would be useful to ask what the president believes that silent majority would want him to do and to how he knows what their views are. If you don't get to ask questions, at least providing context around the protests he referred to such as day of the week, size, and so on are important to include.

CHAPTER 24: THE BIG LIE AND CONSPIRACY THEORIES

1. Voter suppression is bad, but it is truly difficult to know its effects. Removing particular types of voters from voter rolls would influence who voted, but other factors like voter fatigue and even the weather on Election Day can also affect turnout and ultimately the outcome, but this isn't really provable. So is Harris's statement true? We can't say but saying it loud and proud makes it sound like more of a sure thing—a potential example of a Big Lie. The problem with repeating Big Lie statements, even with corrective context, is that the repetition in itself keeps it in the top of mind for some in the audience. If the changes in the voter rolls were an essential part of the story and Harris's views were salient, you would need to provide context. For example, "Harris spoke on the effect of voter suppression on black candidates in the South, stating that suppression was the reason both Stacey Abrams and Andrew Gillum failed in their gubernatorial bids. There's no direct evidence of a connection, but Florida and Georgia did both remove minority voters from their lists of those registered."

2. Repeating quotes like this that are known to be incorrect has the effect of bringing information to public attention and can be a way that journalists and citizens actually spread the Big Lie and make it more effective. Spike Lee is a well-known, award-winning director and, both at the time and today, would be a newsmaker. You could responsibly use the quote in a context piece about misinformation about HIV/AIDS at the time or in a historical piece today. In a story about how a person says an outrageous thing, it would be better to use a highly summarized and also contextualized version of his information. For example, "Spike Lee was quoted in a Benetton advertisement saying that AIDS was a disease created to reduce the black population—a claim for which there is no evidence."

Appendix 3

Possible Answers to Section 3 Exercises

CHAPTER 25: IGNORING THE BASE RATE

1. Sorkin is basing his argument on the large amount of ammunition that Mateen bought and possibly the purchase of two guns for one person. Is that actually unusual, though? Later news reports did note that Mateen bought the guns he used legally. Sorkin is assuming the purchases are out of the ordinary. Are they? Is it, in fact, out of the ordinary to buy that much ammunition at one time? Context would really help in this case. It would be useful to be able to quote statistics on ammunition round purchases per capita (the National Shooting Sports Federation might be a place to start) to see if that amount were uncommon. It would also be interesting to find the cost of those guns and ammunition as a way to let readers make their own comparisons to see if that purchase size is unusual. Sorkin may be right, but it is still helpful to provide additional context.

CHAPTER 26: FALSE CAUSE

1. The statement is implying that increasing years of education caused a diminished sex life. However, the causation isn't clear from the text. For it to be known to be true, you would have to know that the education came first and the diminished sex life followed. In the context of a story, it would be better to report it as there being a relationship between the two. You would also want to ask your source if they had other possible causes and how they controlled for those.

2. Unemployment was, in fact, at a low, but was this reduced unemployment a consequence of accomplishments by the Trump administration? Looking at the rate of unemployment over the time reported,

it's clear that there was a consistent downward trend for years prior to Trump taking office. That doesn't necessarily mean that the Trump administration did not take actions that encouraged hiring, but it is not proven from this trend. You would want to ask for specifics of what actions have been taken. The context of the continuing downward trend would be important to note as context in a story.

CHAPTER 27: THE HIDDEN VARIABLE

1. Sometimes the claims go too far. Godoy's article makes it clear that the wording about the cereal was deceptive. The study, which the cereal company paid for, found improvement for only some children, not most of them. Because the statement was that children who ate the cereal improved by almost 20 percent, that's technically true; there were, in fact, some children in the study who improved that much. It's deceptive because it wasn't most of them. A first question to ask would be who paid for the study, so you can consider if the way it was conducted and interpreted is likely free of bias. If not, asking for original data or another independent source of confirmation is needed.

There was a second level of deceptiveness, though, because the comparison group was not children who ate other foods for breakfast but children who did not eat at all. Eating or not eating breakfast is the Hidden Variable that explains the improvement in attentiveness that some children showed. This was too much deceptiveness for the courts and regulators to take. Angry parents filed a class action lawsuit against the cereal manufacturer and Kellogg's eventually agreed to a $4 million settlement to provide refunds to parents who felt that they had been duped.

2. It's unlikely that paintings do actually cause fires, but are there Hidden Variables that can explain the painting being in so many house fires and in some surviving relatively unscathed? There are. The first would be the popularity of the paintings. If many homeowners had that painting (and in fact, more than 50,000 were sold according to Punt [2010]), then homes that burn would be likely to have them, so the Hidden Variable is popularity. The other question is why the painting often survived. You'd wonder if it was just this painting that tended to survive fires, and the answer to that is no. Paintings tend to fall off a burning wall facedown, so their subjects are often somewhat protected from the damage wrought by the fire and the effort to extinguish it. The Hidden Variable turns out to be the fact that hanging strings burn quickly.

CHAPTER 28: UNNECESSARY PRECISION

1. Adnan was a highly recognized child at the time of his birth, but despite the sign that hung over his head at the hospital, it's not possible to know what number life he was to come into the world. Babies are born continuously all over the world and sometimes in places that don't keep records. As is common with people and big, round numbers, the birth of a baby in Sarajevo was a symbol of both a population milestone and a hope for a more peaceful future in a region that had endured years of brutal civil war as ethic groups disentangled themselves from a definition derived after World War II that put them into one country. It's not like Secretary General Annan just happened to be there and then ran out and had a banner quickly manufactured in another language. Some media did describe the situation accurately—as a symbolic one.

2. The exact figures around lives to be saved are statistical averages and are not accurate predictions of the benefits of different safety plans. Although they look quite official, they will be more confusing than enlightening to the audience. It would be possible to round the figures to say, "Experts estimate that each year about 850 lives could be saved with the regulators' plan, but the car manufacturers favor a plan that would save less than half that. The regulators could prevent close to 37,000 serious injuries a year, according to the estimates. Again, the plan that car manufacturers support would reduce that figure—the time by about a third."

CHAPTER 29: NAÏVE PROBABILITY AND THE AUDIENCE IT CONFUSES

1. If more people die in New York, the Navy would seem to be the place to be, but that relies on a Naïve Probability understanding of dying. Huff (1954) notes that most of the service members in the Navy would be young people selected in part because they are healthy and ready for the Navy mission. Because these are unlikely to die, any number of deaths might indicate danger. On the other hand, people of all ages and in all states of health live in New York. The comparison isn't really fair, and you need to ask the demographics of sailors so you could make that clear as context in the story.

2. The players in *Deal or No Deal* faced a choice between a smaller, sure thing and a chance at a bigger thing, and the banker seems to be offering something around the average of the values of the remaining cases. Although Naïve Probability might tell you that the chances of a

bigger payout make it worth it to keep picking, players forget that they began the game with no money. (However, not all choices are mathematical ones. The entertainment value of playing the game might be worth essentially paying for in reduced chances of the big payout.)

CHAPTER 30: DECEPTION WITH CHARTS

The visualization of the path of a hurricane is a complicated one, and it can be a matter of life and death to contextualize it correctly for the public. The wide path in the map represents uncertainty and gets wider as it tries to predict the future. However, evacuating the population of a crowded metropolitan area can take days, and people need advance warning to be able to secure their property. There is also the question of public trust. If people evacuate needlessly, they may not trust the next forecast and make the life-preserving decision. The strategy for contextualizing, then, is important. The writer can make the point that these are probability-driven estimates of where they eye of the storm might go and that it's wrong to interpret the cone as the storm moving up the middle and spreading. The writer can also continue to report the size of the storm to make the point that even those not in the graphic still may have serious effects from the storm.

CHAPTER 31: MISREPRESENTING POLLS AND SURVEYS

Although the poll results do mostly show Clinton with a lead over Trump, they don't actually indicate that Clinton was a sure thing to win. The percentage leads are not large, suggesting that error alone can make the outcome uncertain. A second factor could be that you don't know the confidence interval. Some of these results could be in the times out of 100 that the results wouldn't be within the predicted range anyway. The best way to describe these results is too close to predict.

References

"Anti-Suffrage Flier, Circa 1918." NewseumED. Accessed October 21, 2019. https://newseumed.org/artifact/anti-suffrage-flier-circa1918/?form_id=12

Barry, Dave. "How to Argue." DaveBarry.com. Accessed October 15, 2019. http://www.davebarry.com/natterings_files/daveHOWTOARGUE.pdf

Boehner, John. Obamacare Not Ready for Prime Time. *Congressional Record*, Vol. 159, No. 132 (House of Representatives, September 30, 2013).

Borrelli, Christopher. "Reagan Used Her, the Country Hated Her. Decades Later, the Welfare Queen of Chicago Refuses to Go Away." chicagotribune.com, June 10, 2019. https://www.chicagotribune.com/entertainment/ct-ent-welfare-queen-josh-levin-0610-story.html

Brainard, Curtis. "Probability Problems." *Columbia Journalism Review*, May 22, 2009. https://archives.cjr.org/the_observatory/probability_problems.php

Braun, Ken. "Ken Braun: Ronald Reagan Might Not Pass Tea Party Scrutiny Being Applied to NJ Gov. Chris Christie." mlive, November 6, 2013. http://www.mlive.com/politics/index.ssf/2013/11/ken_braun_ronald_reagan_might.html

Bump, Philip. "Jim Inhofe's Snowball Has Disproven Climate Change Once and for All." *Washington Post*, April 26, 2019. https://www.washingtonpost.com/news/the-fix/wp/2015/02/26/jim-inhofes-snowball-has-disproven-climate-change-once-and-for-all/

Bush, George W. "President Bush Meets with President Torrijos of Panama." National Archives and Records Administration, November 7, 2005. https://georgewbush-whitehouse.archives.gov/news/releases/2005/11/20051107.html

———. "Remarks to the Veterans of Foreign Wars National Convention, Salt Lake City, Utah." Office of the Federal Register, National Archives and Records Service, and General Services Administration. "Weekly Compilation of Presidential Documents, Volume 19, Issue 2." Google Books. https://books.google.com/books/about/Weekly_Compilation_of_Presidential_Docum.html?id=7dJKAQAAIAAJ

———. "President Bush Outlines Iraqi Threat." National Archives and Records Administration, October 7, 2002. https://georgewbush-whitehouse.archives.gov/news/releases/2002/10/text/20021007-8.html

Cairo, Alberto. *The Truthful Art: Data, Charts, and Maps for Communication.* San Francisco, CA: New Riders, 2016.

"Can You Give Me Some Tips for Maximizing My Las Vegas Buffet Experience?" Las Vegas Advisor. Accessed November 10, 2019. https://www.lasvegasadvisor .com/faq-dining-buffet-tips/

Capaldi, Nicholas. *The Art of Deception*. Santa Monica, CA: DW Brown, 1971.

Carter, James. "Universal Declaration of Human Rights: Remarks at a White House Meeting Commemorating the 30th Anniversary of the Declaration's Signing. Public papers of presidents of the Presidents of the United States." US Federal Register Division, National Archives and Records Service, General Services Administration, December 31, 1978.

Castillo, Michelle. "Planking: How the Potentially Dangerous Trend Is Taking over the Twittersphere." CBS News. CBS Interactive, June 29, 2011. https://www .cbsnews.com/news/planking-how-the-potentially-dangerous-trend-is-taking-over -the-twittersphere/

Cavender, Nancy M., and Howard Kahane. *Logic and Contemporary Rhetoric: The Use of Reason in Everyday Life*. Boston, MA: Cengage Learning, 2009.

"Clinton: 'Rocky' and I Aren't Quitters." CNN. Accessed August 3, 2019. https:// edition.cnn.com/2008/POLITICS/04/01/democrats.pa/

Clinton, Bill J. 1996 State of the Union Address. *Washington Post*, January 23, 1996. https://www.washingtonpost.com/wp-srv/politics/special/states/docs/sou96 .htm

CNBC. "CNBC Transcript of 'Your Money, Your Vote' Republican Presidential Debate." CNBC, November 10, 2011. https://www.cnbc.com/id/45232734

CNN. "Transcript of Thursday's Democratic Presidential Debate." CNN, 2008. https://www.cnn.com/2008/POLITICS/01/31/dem.debate.transcript/

Cohen, Stuart. "Australians Urge U.S. To Look At Their Gun Laws." NPR, December 21, 2012. https://www.npr.org/2012/12/21/167814684/australians-urge-u-s-to -look-at-their-gun-laws

C-SPAN. "Michael Cohen on President Trump: 'He Is a Racist. He Is a Con Man. He Is a Cheat.'" C-span.org. C-SPAN, February 28, 2018. https://www.c-span.org/ video/?458125-1/michael-cohen-president-trump-he-racist-con-man-cheat

Cummins, Denise D., and Colin Allen. *The Evolution of Mind*. Oxford: University Press, 1998.

Damer, T. Edward. *Attacking Faulty Reasoning: a Practical Guide to Fallacy-Free Arguments*. Australia: Wadsworth, Cengage Learning, 2013.

Debonis, Mike. "Republicans Defend Trump after Comey Hearing, Say He's 'New at This,' but Mark Sanford Thinks It's a Weak Excuse." *Post and Courier*, June 8, 2017. https://www.postandcourier.com/news/republicans-defend-trump-after -comey-hearing-say-he-s-new/article_a18bc0f0-4ca0-11e7-b600-af6ffcea56c6 .html

"Do Democrats Want to Take Away Americans' Hamburgers?" BBC News. BBC, March 1, 2019. https://www.bbc.com/news/world-us-canada-47394484

Farzan, Antonia N. "Democrats Want 'What Stalin Dreamt about': Take Away Americans' Hamburgers, Former Trump Aide Says." *Chicago Tribune*, March 1, 2019. https://www.chicagotribune.com/nation-world/ct-cpac-take-away-your -hamburgers-20190301-story.html

Fazio, Victor H. Congressional Record Daily Edition, 138th *Congressional Record Daily Edition* §. Accessed November 25, 2019. https://congressional.proquest

.com.ezproxy.elon.edu/congressional/result/congressional/congdocumentview
?accountid=10730&groupid=105293&parmId=16E28E7F9C3

Flagg, Anna. "Is There a Connection Between Undocumented Immigrants and Crime?" *New York Times*, May 13, 2019. https://www.nytimes.com/2019/05/13/upshot/illegal-immigration-crime-rates-research.html

Fuller, Jack. *News Values: Ideas for an Information Age*. Chicago: University of Chicago Press, 1997.

"George W Bush on the Tribal Sovereignty—2004." C-SPAN. Accessed July 1, 2019. https://www.c-span.org/video/?c4672207/user-clip-george-bush-tribal-sovereignty-2004

Godoy, Maria. "No, Frosted Mini-Wheats Won't Make Your Kids Smarter." NPR, May 30, 2013. https://www.npr.org/sections/thesalt/2013/05/30/187330235/no-frosted-mini-wheats-don-t-make-your-kids-smarter

Gomez, Melissa. "Giuliani Says 'Truth Isn't Truth' in Defense of Trump's Legal Strategy." *New York Times*, August 19, 2018. https://www.nytimes.com/2018/08/19/us/giuliani-meet-the-press-truth-is-not-truth.html

Greenberg, Jon. "Bernie Sanders: U.S. 'Only Major Country' That Doesn't Guarantee Right to Health Care." @politifact, June 29, 2015. https://www.politifact.com/truth-o-meter/statements/2015/jun/29/bernie-s/bernie-sanders-us-only-major-country-doesnt-guaran/

Gutierrez, Melanie. "Opponents Call It a 'Crime against Humanity,' but Vaccine Bill Moves Forward." *Los Angeles Times*, April 25, 2019. https://www.latimes.com/politics/la-pol-ca-vaccine-exemption-review-bill-20190424-story.html

Guynn, Jessica. "Ted Cruz Threatens to Regulate Facebook, Google and Twitter over Charges of Anti-Conservative Bias." *USA Today*, April 10, 2019. https://www.usatoday.com/story/news/2019/04/10/ted-cruz-threatens-regulate-facebook-twitter-over-alleged-bias/3423095002/

Haag, Matthew, and Maya Salam. "Gunman in 'Pizzagate' Shooting Is Sentenced to 4 Years in Prison." *New York Times*, June 23, 2017. https://www.nytimes.com/2017/06/22/us/pizzagate-attack-sentence.html

Hannity, Sean. "Sean Hannity: Democrats Use Vegas Tragedy to Undermine Constitution." FOX News Network, October 6, 2017. https://www.foxnews.com/opinion/sean-hannity-democrats-use-vegas-tragedy-to-undermine-constitution

Heller, Jacob. "Rumors and Realities: Making Sense of HIV/AIDS Conspiracy Narratives and Contemporary Legends." *American Journal of Public Health* 105, no. 1 (2015). https://doi.org/10.2105/ajph.2014.302284.

Hernandez, Salvador. "A Man Has Been Charged with Trying to Burn Down the Restaurant at the Center of the 'Pizzagate' Conspiracy." BuzzFeed News, February 14, 2019. https://www.buzzfeednews.com/article/salvadorhernandez/pizzagate-conspiracy-comet-ping-pong-fire-dc-arrest

Hines, Ree. "Poor Daniel Baldwin! Lesser Celebrity Siblings." TODAY.com, December 16, 2008. https://www.today.com/popculture/poor-daniel-baldwin-lesser-celebrity-siblings-wbna28256516

Historical perspective [This Dynamic Earth, USGS]. Accessed December 1, 2019. https://pubs.usgs.gov/gip/dynamic/historical.html.

Hitler, Adolf. *Mein Kampf: My Struggle: Four and a Half Years of Struggle against Lies, Stupidity, and Cowardice*. Stone Mountain, GA: White Wolf, 2014.

Hook, Janet. "Frist Plagued Again by Comments on Schiavo." *Los Angeles Times*, June 17, 2005. https://www.latimes.com/archives/la-xpm-2005-jun-17-na-frist17 -story.html.

Huff, Darrell. *How to Lie with Statistics*. New York: Norton, 1954.

Hutzler, Alexandra. "Kamala Harris Said That without Voter Suppression, Stacey Abrams and Andrew Gillum Would've Won Their 2018 Races." *Newsweek*, May 6, 2019. https://www.newsweek.com/kamala-harris-voter-suppression-abrams -gillum-1415903

"Iran Nuclear Deal: Key Details." BBC News. BBC, June 11, 2019. https://www.bbc .com/news/world-middle-east-33521655

Jaramillo, Cassandra. "Dallas' Curfew on Kids Could Come Back Sooner than You Think." *Dallas News*. Dallas News, August 23, 2019. https://www.dallasnews .com/news/2019/01/23/dallas-curfew-on-kids-could-come-back-sooner-than -you-think/

Johnson, Lyndon B. *Lyndon B. Johnson: 1968–1969 (in Two Books): Containing the Public Messages, Speeches, and Statements of the President*. Washington: Office of the Federal Register, National Archives and Records Service, General Services Administration, 1970.

Jones, Gerald E. *How to Lie with Charts*. Santa Monica, CA: LaPuerta, 2015.

Kennedy, John F. "Senator John F. Kennedy and Vice President Richard M. Nixon First Joint Radio-Television Broadcast, September 26, 1960." JFK Library. Accessed October 24, 2019. https://www.jfklibrary.org/archives/other-resources/ john-f-kennedy-speeches/1st-nixon-kennedy-debate-19600926.

———. "John F. Kennedy, The Berlin Crisis." John F. Kennedy, The Berlin Crisis—July 25, 1961. Presidential Rhetoric.com, July 25, 1961. http://presidential rhetoric.com/historicspeeches/kennedy/berlincrisis.html

———. Inaugural Address, January 20, 1961. http://www2.york.psu.edu/~jmj3/ kennedy.htm

Kesslen, Ben. "South Dakota's 'Meth. We're on It.' Campaign Is Funny but State Officials Say the Meth Problem Is Deadly Serious." NBCNews.com, November 20, 2019. https://www.nbcnews.com/news/us-news/south-dakota-s-meth-we-re-it -campaign-funny-state-n1086071

Kessler, Glenn. "Clinton's Claim That the Bush Tax Cuts Played 'a Large Part' in Sparking 2008 Recession." *Washington Post*, August 15, 2018. https://www .washingtonpost.com/news/fact-checker/wp/2016/09/30/clintons-claim-that-the -bush-tax-cuts-played-a-large-part-in-sparking-2008-recession/

———. "Analysis | History Lesson: How the Democrats Pushed Obamacare through the Senate." *Washington Post*, August 15, 2018. https://www.washingtonpost .com/news/fact-checker/wp/2017/06/22/history-lesson-how-the-democrats -pushed-obamacare-through-the-senate/

Knox, Bryant. "USA Olympic Basketball Team 2012: Roster, Complete Schedule and More." *Bleacher Report*. Bleacher Report, September 25, 2017. https://bleacher report.com/articles/1271311-usa-olympic-basketball-team-2012-roster-complete -schedule-and-more

Kurtzleben, Danielle. "With 'Fake News,' Trump Moves from Alternative Facts to Alternative Language." NPR, February 18, 2017. https://www.npr.org/2017/02/

17/515630467/with-fake-news-trump-moves-from-alternative-facts-to-alternative
-language

"Law, Facts, & Hostile Judges." Class Action Countermeasures, August 27, 2018.
https://www.classactioncountermeasures.com/2014/03/articles/scholarship/
law-facts-hostile-judges/

Levin, Bess. "United C.E.O. Offers the Worst Possible Response to the Airline's P.R.
Disaster." *Vanity Fair*, April 11, 2017. https://www.vanityfair.com/news/2017/04/
united-airlines-oscar-munoz

Mattes, Richard D. "Prevention of Food Aversions in Cancer Patients during
Treatment." *Nutrition and Cancer* 21, no. 1 (1994): 13–24. https://doi.org/
10.1080/01635589409514300

McDowell, Simone. "Conversations to Have before You Say 'I Do,' According to a
Premarital Counselor." *The Charlotte Observer*, March 22, 2017. https://www
.charlotteobserver.com/charlottefive/c5-people/article236167323.html

McGregor, Jena. "Analysis | From 'Tone-Deaf' to 'Textbook': Experts Review the
United CEO's First—and Latest—Apology." *Washington Post*, April 7, 2019.
https://www.washingtonpost.com/news/on-leadership/wp/2017/04/11/from-tone
-deaf-to-textbook-experts-review-the-united-ceos-first-and-latest-apology/

McNerney, Jerry. Climate Change Caused by Human Activity. *Congressional Record*
Vol. 159, No. 132 (House of Representatives, September 30, 2013)

Moskowitz, P. E. *The Case against Free Speech: The First Amendment, Fascism, and
the Future of Dissent*. New York: Bold Type Books, 2019.

MSNBC. "Christine Blasey Ford Describes Sexual Assault. Transcript: 9/27/2018,
The Rachel Maddow Show." MSNBC. NBCUniversal News Group, September
27, 2018. http://www.msnbc.com/transcripts/rachel-maddow-show/2018-09-27

Mulvihill, Geoff. "Q&A: Census Citizenship Question Sparks Legal Debate,
Fears." Associated Press, June 24, 2019. https://apnews.com/4757a2f6546b45
938c31e00937ba7f78

"Museum of the Flat Earth." *Atlas Obscura*, March 6, 2018. https://www.atlas
obscura.com/places/museum-of-the-flat-earth

Nakamura, David. "Obama: 8 Million Have Signed up for Health Care." *Washington Post*, May 1, 2019. https://www.washingtonpost.com/news/post-politics/
wp/2014/04/17/obama-8-million-have-signed-up-for-health-care/

"National Marriage Project: Research and Analysis on the Health of Marriage in
America." The National Marriage Project. Accessed November 15, 2019. http://
nationalmarriageproject.org/

"Nazis, Skokie and the A.C.L.U." *New York Times*, January 1, 1978. https://www
.nytimes.com/1978/01/01/archives/nazis-skokie-and-the-aclu.html

Nixon, Richard. "Public Papers of the Presidents." National Archives and Records
Administration, November 3, 1969. https://www.archives.gov/federal-register/
publications/presidential-papers.html

Noah, Timothy. "Bill Clinton and the Meaning of 'Is.'" *Slate Magazine*, September 14, 1998. https://slate.com/news-and-politics/1998/09/bill-clinton-and-the
-meaning-of-is.html

"Obama's False Dichotomy of the Iran Nuclear Deal." Council on Foreign Relations.
Accessed October 1, 2019. https://www.cfr.org/blog/obamas-false-dichotomy
-iran-nuclear-deal

"October 11, 2000 Debate Transcript." CPD: October 11, 2000 Debate Transcript. Accessed August 4, 2019. https://www.debates.org/voter-education/debate-transcripts/october-11-2000-debate-transcript/

Pengelly, Martin. "Rick Santorum: US Is 'Moral Leader of World' in Fight against Gay Marriage." *The Guardian*, July 5, 2015. https://www.theguardian.com/us-news/2015/jul/05/rick-santorum-same-sex-marriage-moral

Peralta, Eyder. "Obama: It's Not Bigger Government We Need, It's A 'Smarter' One." NPR, February 12, 2013. https://www.npr.org/sections/itsallpolitics/2013/02/07/171410659/live-blog-president-obamas-state-of-the-union-address

Pessin, Andrew, and S. Morris Engel. *The Study of Philosophy: a Text with Readings*. Lanham, MD: Rowman & Littlefield, 2015.

Politico Staff. "Presidential Debate Transcript, Questions, Oct. 16, 2012 (Text, Video)." Politico. Accessed December 1, 2019. https://www.politico.com/news/stories/1012/82484_Page4.html

Proceedings of 18th National Convention of the American Legion, Cleveland, Ohio, Sept. 21–24, 1936 (1937).

Pruitt, Sarah. "Ted Kennedy's Chappaquiddick Incident: What Really Happened." History.com. A&E Television Networks, April 6, 2018. https://www.history.com/news/ted-kennedy-chappaquiddick-incident-what-really-happened-facts

Pugmire, Tim. "Bachmann, Tinklenberg Clash in Debate." MPR News. October 16, 2008. https://www.mprnews.org/story/2008/10/16/bachmann-tinklenberg-clash-in-debate

Punt, Steve. "Solved: Curse of the Crying Boy Comic's Obsession with Painting." October 9, 2010. *The Sun*, p. 8.

Purdum, Todd S. "Clinton Warns of U.S. Retreat To Isolationism." *New York Times*, October 7, 1995. https://www.nytimes.com/1995/10/07/world/clinton-warns-of-us-retreat-to-isolationism.html

Rampell, Catherine. "The Stock Market under Trump vs. Obama." *Washington Post*, March 30, 2019. https://www.washingtonpost.com/news/rampage/wp/2018/05/01/the-stock-market-under-trump-vs-obama/

Rathi, Akshat. "A Cambridge Professor on How to Stop Being so Easily Manipulated by Misleading Statistics." *Quartz*, March 27, 2016. https://qz.com/643234/cambridge-professor-on-how-to-stop-being-so-easily-manipulated-by-misleading-statistics/

Robinson, Rashad. "We Can't Trust Police to Protect Us from Racist Violence. They Contribute to It." *The Guardian*, August 21, 2019. https://www.theguardian.com/commentisfree/2019/aug/21/police-white-nationalists-racist-violence

Roy, Jessica. "As the Russia Investigation Continues, Art Buchwald's Nixon Excuses Column Resurfaces." *Los Angeles Times*, July 19, 2019. https://www.latimes.com/newsletters/todaysheadlines/la-na-essential-washingto-updates-201707-htmlstory.html#as-the-russia-investigation-continues-art-buchwalds-nixon-excuses-column-resurfaces

"Rubio Bashes Trump, Clinton and Sanders; Insults Fly as Trump and Rubio Escalate Attacks; The Latino Factor; Democrats Vote in South Carolina Primary; Donald Trump Holds Rally Days Before Super Tuesday." CNN, February 27, 2016. http://www.cnn.com/TRANSCRIPTS/1602/27/cnr.04.html

Sacramento Bee. "Notable Quotes from Gov. Arnold Schwarzenegger." sacbee. *Sacramento Bee*, October 3, 2008. https://www.sacbee.com/news/politics-government/article2572282.html

Scott, Eugene. "Why Ted Cruz Was Making a Biblical Case for Gun Rights after the Odessa Shooting." *Washington Post*, September 4, 2019. https://www.washingtonpost.com/politics/2019/09/04/why-ted-cruz-was-making-biblical-case-gun-rights-after-odessa-shooting/

"Secretary-General to Welcome 6 Billionth World Citizen." United Nations, October 11, 1999. https://www.un.org/press/en/1999/19991011.sg2061.doc.html

Sessions, Jefferson. "Attorney General Sessions Delivers Remarks at the Department of Justice's Religious Liberty Summit." The US Department of Justice, July 31, 2018. https://www.justice.gov/opa/speech/attorney-general-sessions-delivers-remarks-department-justice-s-religious-liberty-summit

Silver, Nate. "Election Update: Don't Ignore The Polls—Clinton Leads, But It's A Close Race." FiveThirtyEight. FiveThirtyEight, November 6, 2016. https://fivethirtyeight.com/features/election-update-dont-ignore-the-polls-clinton-leads-but-its-a-close-race/

Sorkin, Andrew Ross. "How Banks Could Control Gun Sales If Washington Won't." *New York Times*, February 20, 2018. https://www.nytimes.com/2018/02/19/business/banks-gun-sales.html

Spicer, Robert N. "Lies, Damn Lies, Alternative Facts, Fake News, Propaganda, Pinocchios, Pants on Fire, Disinformation, Misinformation, Post-Truth, Data, and Statistics." In *Free Speech and False Speech*, 1–31. London, UK: Palgrave Macmillan, 2018.

Stam, Paul. "SB 514—Defense of Marriage Rep. Paul Stam—Remarks on 2nd Reading." Collection of Debate Transcripts, September 12, 2011. http://paulstam.info/wp-content/uploads/2016/11/Collection-of-Debate-Transcripts-North-Carolina-General-Assembly-2009-2016.pdf

"Study Finds More Educated People Have Sex Less Often." *Chronicle of Higher Education*, January 23, 1998. https://www.chronicle.com/article/Study-Finds-More-Educated/99310

Suebsaeng, Asawin. "Must-Reads: The Late, Great Molly Ivins on Rick Perry." *Mother Jones*, June 25, 2017. https://www.motherjones.com/politics/2011/08/rick-perry-molly-ivins/

"Text: Bush and Daschle Comments on Security and Politics." *New York Times*, September 26, 2002. https://www.nytimes.com/2002/09/26/politics/text-bush-and-daschle-comments-on-security-and-politics.html

Thompson, Derek. "Marissa Mayer Is Wrong: Working From Home Can Make You More Productive." *The Atlantic*. Atlantic Media Company, February 26, 2013. https://www.theatlantic.com/business/archive/2013/02/marissa-mayer-is-wrong-working-from-home-can-make-you-more-productive/273482/

Tickell, Oliver. "Crash Course in Safety." *The Guardian*. Guardian News and Media, July 6, 2005. https://www.theguardian.com/science/2005/jul/07/6

"Transcript of the First TV Debate Between Bush and Dukakis." *New York Times*, September 26, 1988. https://www.nytimes.com/1988/09/26/us/presidential-debate-transcript-first-tv-debate-between-bush-dukakis.html

"Transcript of Thursday's Democratic Presidential Debate." CNN. Accessed October 1, 2019. https://www.cnn.com/2008/POLITICS/01/31/dem.debate.transcript/

Trump, Donald J. "Remarks by President Trump on the Illegal Immigration Crisis and Border Security." The White House. The US government. November 1, 2018. https://www.whitehouse.gov/briefings-statements/remarks-president-trump-illegal-immigration-crisis-border-security/

US Department of Agriculture. "United States Standards, Grades, and Weight Classes for Shell Eggs." *USDA*. n.d. https://www.ams.usda.gov/sites/default/files/media/Shell_Egg_Standard%5B1%5D.pdf

US Department of State. "Soviet Influence Activities: A Report on Active Measures and Propaganda, 1986–87." *Global Security* n.d. https://www.globalsecurity.org/intell/library/reports/1987/soviet-influence-activities-1987.pdf

Verhovek, Sam Howe. "Bush Tax Plan for Texas, and 2000." *New York Times*, January 30, 1997. https://www.nytimes.com/1997/01/30/us/bush-tax-plan-for-texas-and-2000.html

Vigen, Tyler. *Spurious Correlations*. London: Hachette Books, 2015.

Washington Post Staff. "Full Text: Obama Gives a Speech about the Iran Nuclear Deal." *Washington Post*, May 1, 2019. https://www.washingtonpost.com/news/post-politics/wp/2015/08/05/text-obama-gives-a-speech-about-the-iran-nuclear-deal/

"'Welfare Queen' Becomes Issue in Reagan Campaign." *New York Times*, February 15, 1976. https://www.nytimes.com/1976/02/15/archives/welfare-queen-becomes-issue-in-reagan-campaign-hitting-a-nerve-now.html

"WHATABOUTISM: Definition in the Cambridge English Dictionary." WHATABOUTISM | definition in the *Cambridge English Dictionary*. Accessed October 1, 2019. https://dictionary.cambridge.org/us/dictionary/english/whataboutism

"What Clinton Said." *Washington Post*, January 26, 1998. https://www.washingtonpost.com/wp-srv/politics/special/clinton/stories/whatclintonsaid.htm

Wolfensberger, Don. (2014, Sept. 29). "Ding-Dong Bell, Let's Go Poison the Well." *Roll Call*.

Yagoda, Ben. "One Cheer for Whataboutism." *New York Times*, July 19, 2018. https://www.nytimes.com/2018/07/19/opinion/one-cheer-for-whataboutism.html

"'You Are Either with Us or against Us.'" CNN. Accessed October 11, 2019. https://edition.cnn.com/2001/US/11/06/gen.attack.on.terror/

Zarrelli, Natalie. "A Painting of a Crying Boy Was Blamed for a Series of Fires in the '80s." *Atlas Obscura*, June 2, 2017. https://www.atlasobscura.com/articles/crying-boy-painting-fires

Index

Abrams, Stacey, 85, 136
ad hominem, 4–6
advertising, 32, 94, 97, 138
AFL-CIO 33, 24, 123
algorithms, computer, 66, 90
antitrust lawsuits, 66–67
American Civil Liberties Union
    (ACLU), 26
American Legion, 52
Annan, Kofi, 101, 138
argumentum ad antiquitatem, 77
argumentum ad baculum, 66
argumentum ad misericordiam, 63
argumentum ad ignorantium, 69
argumentum ad populum, 80
argumentum ad vericundiam, 72
Appalachian Trail, 38
appeal to: authority, 72–75, 133–134;
    force, 66–68, 132; hypocrisy,
    14–16, 120; ignorance, 69–71,
    133; pity, 63–65, 131–132;
    popularity, 80–82, 135–136; purity,
    51–53, 128; tradition, 76–79,
    134–135
automobile safety 101, 139

Bachmann, Michelle, 46–47, 126
Baldwin, Alec, 42
Baldwin, Billy, 42
Baldwin, Daniel, 42
Baldwin, Stephen, 42
Barr, Roseanne, 16, 120
Barry, Dave, 99–100
basketball, 46

Bee, Samantha, 5, 16, 120
begging the question, 48–50, 127
Berlin Crisis 68
big lie, 83–85, 136
bin Laden, Osama, 22–23
birth control, 90
black and white, 20–24, 121
Black Lives Matter, 35–36
Blasey Ford, Christine, 15, 120
Blitzer, Wolf, 18, 120
Boehner, John, 8
bots, social media, 84
Bryant, Kobe, 46
Bush, George H.W., 70–71
Bush, George W., 12–13, 16, 23, 40, 49,
    56, 59, 66, 74, 94, 121, 128–129,
    132, 133

calorie counts, 100–101
cancer, 93–94
Carter, Jimmy, 81
Caslen, Robert, 37, 124
Catholicism, 90
Census, US, 113
Chappaquiddick, Massachusetts, 15
Christie, Chris, 52
climate change, 9, 39, 103–104
Clinton, Bill, 13, 55–56, 63–64, 119,
    128, 131
Clinton, Hillary, 18–19, 33–34, 49, 94,
    115, 120, 123, 140
Cohen, Michael, 10–11, 199
Cold War, 68
Comedy Central, 4

Comet Ping Pong Pizza, 84
Comey, James, 65
composition fallacy, 45, 126–127
Congressional Record, 8
Conservative Political Action
    Conference (CPAC), 3
continental drift, 30
Coolidge, Calvin, 48–49
Crying Boy, 97–98
Cruz, Ted, 66, 74–75, 134
curfews, 22
Cummings, Elijah, 10

Daniels, Stormy, 10
Dao, David, 17–8
Deal or No Deal, 104, 139–140
Dean, Richard, 65
deception with charts, 105–110, 140
Dershowitz, Alan, 90–91
dicto simpliciter, 38
division fallacy, 41–44, 125–126
divorce, 103
Dr Pepper, 80
Dukakis, Michael, 70–71, 133
Dunn, Aubert, 52, 128
Durant, Kevin, 46

equivocation, 53–56, 128–129
European Union, 101

fallacy of fallacies, 29–31
false cause, 93–95, 137–138
flat earth, 29–31
Fleischer, Ari, 16, 120
faulty analogy, 32–34, 123–124
Fazio, Vic, 53, 128
Federal Bureau of Investigation (FBI),
    65
Franco, Olga, 46
free speech, 25, 66
Frist, Bill, 74, 133–134

game shows, 104
gay marriage, 70, 78, 134–135
Gillum, Andrew, 85, 136
Goldman, Ronald, 91
Gonzalez, Danny, 80

Gore, Al, 40, 124
Gorka, Sebastian, 3
government shut down, 64, 131
Green New Deal, 3
gun control. *See* Second Amendment
    rights

Haiti, 53, 128
Hannity, Sean, 27, 122
Harris, Kamala, 85, 136
hasty generalization, viii, 38–40, 90,
    125
health care: Affordable Care Act, 8, 13;
    Universal, 82, 135
Hickson, William J., 28, 122
hidden variable, 96–98, 138
Hitler, Adolf, 83
HIV/AIDS, 85, 89, 136
Holocaust, 26
Hussein, Saddam, 66

ignoratio elenchi, 17, 35
ignoring the base rate, 89–92, 137
immigration, 40–41, 46–47, 53,
    125–126, 128
Inhofe, James, 39
Iran Nuclear Deal, 6, 23, 117, 122
irrelevant conclusion, 35–37, 124
Ivins, Molly, 49

James, LeBron, 46
Johnson, Lyndon, 34, 123–124
Jones, Paula, 55
Jordan, Jim, 10–11, 119

Kavanaugh, Brett, 15–16, 120
Kennedy, Edward, 15
Kennedy, John, 10, 50, 68, 118, 127,
    132
Klepper, Jordan, 4
Klobuchar, Amy, 16, 120
Kopechne, Mary Jo, 15

Las Vegas: buffets, 59, 129; slot
    machines, 102
Lee, Spike, 85, 136
Lewinsky, Monica, 55–56, 128

Lieberman, Joe, 52
Lohan, Ali, 40
Lohan, Lindsay, 40
lying press, 4

masculinity, 27, 122
mass shootings, 92
Mateen, Omar, 92, 137
Mayer, Marissa, 78
McCarthy, Joseph, 69–70
McDonald's, 80
McNerney, Jerry, 9
Meany, George, 34
Mevic, Adnan, 101, 138
Milano, Alyssa, 74–75, 134
Muñoz, Oscar, 19

näive probability, 102–104, 139–140
nazis, 26
Nixon, Richard, 10, 16, 82, 118, 135–136
Noah, Trevor, 4
no true Scotsman, 51

Obama, Barack, 6, 13, 16, 18, 23–24, 64, 95, 117, 122
Oklahoma City bombing, 65
O'Reilly, Bill, 46

Pan, Richard, 41, 125
Pauling, Linus, 73
Pelosi, Nancy, 27, 122
Perot, H. Ross, 105
Perry, Rick, 49
personal attack, 4–6, 7, 117–118
planking, 81
Pledge of Allegiance, 77, 133
polls and surveys, interpreting, 90, 140
poisoning the well, 7–11, 118–119
police brutality, 47, 127
poverty, 34, 123–124
push polling, 113

racism, 47
Reagan, Ronald, 40, 124
red herring, viii, 17–20, 120
Reses, Jackie, 78, 135

right to die, 73–74
Robinson, Rashad, 47
Rocky, 33, 123
Romney, Mitt, 19–20, 36, 121, 124
Roosevelt, Franklin, 52, 128
Rubio, Marco, 50, 127
Ryan, Paul, 65, 131–132

Sanders, Bernie, 82, 135
Santorum, Rick, 78, 134–135
Saturday Night Live, 118
Schaefer, Matthew, 74–75, 134
Schaivo, Michael, 73
Schaivo, Terry, 73–74, 133–134
Schwarzenegger, Arnold, 6, 118
Second Amendment rights, 27, 40, 63–64, 74, 122, 124, 134, 137
Sessions, Jeff, 90
Simpson, Nicole, 91
Simpson, O.J., 90–91
silent majority, 82
slippery slope, 25–28, 122–123
social media, 66
Society of Professional Journalists Code of Ethics, vii
Spanish-American War, 104
Stam, Paul, 70, 133
Stephens, Bret, 27
Stewart, Jon, 4
straw man, 12–13, 119
sudden infant death syndrome, 77
suffrage, 27–28
sunk cost, 57–59, 129

Tea Party, 51
terrorism: global, 39, 121; September 11 attacks, 22–23, 56, 59, 67
Timex, 80
Trump, Donald, 10, 40–41, 49, 50, 65, 66, 95, 115, 119, 120, 125–126, 131–132, 137–138, 140
Trump, Ivanka, 16
Trump, Melania, 10
tu quoque, 15

unemployment, 95, 107–109, 137–138
United Airlines, 17–18

2198231970008 56

United Nations, 13
University of South Carolina, 37,
    124
unnecessary precision, 99–101, 138
U.S. House of Representatives, 8

vaccination, 41, 126
Veterans of Foreign Wars, 59, 141
Vietnam War, 15, 82, 135–136

War on Terror, 59
waterboarding, 56, 128–129
West Point, 124
Wegener, Alfred, 30
welfare, 40, 124
Wikileaks, 84
women, binders full of, 19, 121

Yahoo!, 78, 135